1752

Coat of Arms of the Clelands of that Ilk.

Signatures of James Cleland of that Ilk, of Alexander his son and heir, of James his brother, and of Claud Cleland, appended to a deed dated 1626.

THE

ANCIENT FAMILY OF

CLELAND.

BEING

An Account of the Clelands of that Ilk, in the
County of Lanark ; of the Branches of Faskine,
Monkland, etc. ; and of others of the name.

COMPILED FROM THE RECORDS

BY

JOHN BURTON CLELAND.

Printed by
HICKS. WILKINSON & SEARS,
4, DORSET BUILDINGS, FLEET STREET, LONDON.

1905.

PREFACE.

THIS account is to be considered more as a compilation from various records than a narrative history of the family. There has been no warping of truth to accomplish any end. The authority for each statement is cited, and where hypothetical speculation has been necessary the value to be attached to it has, as far as possible, been estimated. Such work as this will be considered by many but as labour in vain. Still it must be remembered that we all are, in great part, what our forbears made us, and, by looking into the annals of the past, traits of the present and glimpses of the future may often be discerned amidst those dusty records. And surely the pride of the old French nobleman, who said,

"Ni prince, ni roi je suis
Je suis le sieur de Coucy."

is one to be commended, carrying with it as it does the nobler attributes of a hatred of all infamy and deceit, and a striving after the highest ideals of knighthood. May the perusal, then, of these pages not only show us what our forefathers did and how they lived, but also raise in us a desire to uphold to the uttermost the honour of the fair name that once was theirs and now is ours, and which we hold in trust for generations yet to come.

" Avoid foolish questions and genealogies and contentions and striving about the law, for they are unprofitable and vain."

CONTENTS.

THE ANCIENT FAMILY OF CLELAND.

" A DESCRIPTION of the Ancient Family of Cleland in the County of Lanark :—The Hare is carried in arms by an old family with us of the name of Cleland of that Ilk in the County of Lanark; 'tis said they were hereditary Foresters to the old Earls of Douglas, which gave rise to their Arms." (*Nisbet's Heraldry. 1722.*) The principal Arms of the Family are :—" Azure; A Hare saliant argent, with a Hunting-Horn, Vert, hanging about its neck, garnished, gules · Crest, A Falcon standing upon a left hand Glove, proper. Motto, Non Sibi; at other times, For Sport, supported by Two Grey-Hounds, as in the Lion's Register, and Plate of Achievments." (*Nisbet.*)

" The family of Cleland is of great antiquity in Scotland. Their Coat-of-Arms, tradition states, was acquired by their being hereditary foresters to the ancient Earls of Douglas." (*Document.*)

" The old name of the family was Kneland, or Kneiland, now softened into Cleland. There has been a diversity of opinion about the origin of the name of the estate, and to avoid theorizing, I will give the old name—Clelandtoun—which signifies Cleland's dwelling or residence. From this rendering it would appear that the family name was given to the estate, a custom prevalent at an early date The Clelands were an ancient family of distinction as early as the reign of Alexander III., and their history, like that of other old families, is involved in obscurity and error; . . . . both the family and estate have been so long split and divided, that it would require long and diligent research to give a complete history of these divisions." (*Grossart's " History of the Parish of Shotts." 1880.*)

The name is supposed to be derived from the German " knecht " (the same word as our " knight "), a servant. Knechtland would be one who for his land served the king in peace or war, one serving for land : or perhaps it means servant of the land, the land-servant, the family who were hereditary land-servants or foresters of the Earls of Douglas.

The suggested derivation from "Clay-land" is, of course, absurd. A recent suggestion that the name is a corruption of Fillan (or rather that Cleland and St. Fillan are names with a common ancestry, shared by Gilfillan and MacClelland) deserves consideration, especially since there is a St. Fillan's well or spring in the river near Cleland House

"So that those, it seems, who were qualified to be admitted to Justs and Tournaments, though but Gentlemen, had Right to carry supporters; but now they are allowed to none under the Dignity of a Lord-Baron, except those who have right to them by Prescription." *(Nisbet's Heraldry. 1722.)* This shows the distinction of the coat-of-arms of the Clelands, the supporters being still carried by the head of the name.

"One of the oldest and most distinguished families in Clydesdale" *(Writer in "Notes and Queries" 1866.)*

CLELAND TOWN, which derived its name from being the seat of the Clelands, lies some few miles north of Wishaw and about ten east of Glasgow Though at one time a pretty and picturesque country village, the discovery of coal in its neighbourhood has altered all these characteristics. It consists of two roads crossing each other at right angles, and lined on each side by small gray cottages and larger closes Around it are numerous works and collieries with their blackening chimney-stacks, and railway-lines cross in all directions. A resident informed me that he knew of no Clelands in the neighbourhood, the last (who inhabited a farm on the way to Wishaw) "died out some while back"; all others were likewise "dead and gone."

CLELAND HOUSE —"The first remarkable house we meet with upon this water of South Calder, after it enters the parish of Bothwell is the House of Cleland. This is a very good house, antiently the seat of the Clelands of that ilk; but now it belongs to Alexander Inglis, alias Hamilton Murdoston, son to Gavin Hamilton, late one of the under Clerks of Session. It is situate upon the north bank of South Calder. It stands upon a rock with a precipice towards the water. There is here a great deall of wood, and some regular planting. In the rock below the house, toward the water, there is a naturall cave capable to contain forty or fifty men. The bearing of this house from the kirk is N.E. at near four miles distance. It lyes two miles south from Lachop. . . . At the lower end of Cleland wood stands the mill of Cleland, upon the water of Calder." *(William Hamilton, Incumbent of Bothwell Parish, in his "Description of Paroch of*

Bothwell." *1720)* " About half a mile above that (*i e.,* Carfine) is Cleland, the seat of Laird of Cleland; very old and the chief of that name. It is a good house with convenient gardens, woods, inclosers, and coall." *(William Hamilton of Wishaw. 1710)*

Cleland House is situated on the bank of the South Calder between Cleland and Motherwell, about three quarters of a mile from the former and one and a half from the latter. The late owner, Mr Colville, has built a stone wall and gate at the entrance ; an avenue leads a few hundred yards between trees and an undergrowth of ferns, and then runs across a turfy field, being bounded by iron railings and having the pit of a large colliery on the left. The house itself is a large square building, faced by a lawn and surrounded by a park containing fine old trees. Two or three minutes' walk from the house one reaches a precipitous bank, at the bottom of which the South Calder runs, tumbling and foaming—this is the " Glen," a wild and romantic spot, and here is a cave, said to be Wallace's Cave, where the hero at one time took hiding. Some few years ago this spot narrowly escaped destruction by a landslip The sides of the Glen are well covered with trees and luxuriant in ferns The house itself has been apparently much altered and restored by its later proprietors; it is of two storeys. A passage runs parallel to the front into which the hall leads; the front side of this passage is occupied by dining, drawing and public rooms, while behind the passage-way are various offices. The rooms are fine and large and the ceilings very artistically decorated. Though Cleland House and Estate is a rural and pretty spot, yet the atmosphere is heavy with smoke from neighbouring chimney-stacks, and the air full of the whirr of machinery and blowing of whistles.

There is, of course, no record of the acquisition of the estate by the family, the name " Cleland " only being given to it after the family had settled there, certainly considerably before the middle of the thirteenth century The first sale of the estate probably occurred about 1640 by the son of Alexander of the 14th generation, to the " cousin of his own name." The second sale occurred in 1702, when this cousin " sold and dispensed Cleland estate to William and Archibald Hamilton, for behoot of his creditors, and in 1711 it was sold by public roup and purchased by Gavin Hamilton of Moerdovat, for the sum of £29,185 5s 8d Scots money, being £2,432 sterling." The third sale occurred " in 1766 from Alexander Inglis Hamilton of Murdoston to Captain

Hew Dalrymple of Fordal foi £6,310 sterling." The last sale took place about 1900, when Mr. Colville bought the estate indirectly from the Hon. — Dalrymple, brother of the Earl of Stair, for £56,000. He died the next year, and his widow now owns it. The coal found on the estate is said to be the best in Lanarkshire. Some while ago, the company leasing the colliery on it offered to rebuild Cleland House if they might be allowed to mine the rich coal seam underlying it.

" In the parish of Shotts, on the north bank of one of the streams called Calder, in the middle of the steep rock upon which the house of Cleland stands, is a large natural cave which had been partly improved by art, capable of holding forty or fifty men, of difficult access. The entry was secured by a door and an iron gate fixed in the solid rock. The fireplace and part of the chimney and floor still remain. The tradition is that it had been used as a place of concealment in the troublesome times of the country, as far back as the gallant patriot Sir William Wallace, perhaps by the hero himself and his trusty band; also during the violent feuds between the houses of Cleland and Lauchope; and especially in the convulsions of this country under the last of the Stuarts." *(" The Beauties of Scotland," by Robt. Forsyth. Constable, Edinburgh. 1806)*

" The late Robert Craig had a saying that every true Cleland should have a crooked mouth because once upon a time the laird sat on the roof of his house when who should appear but the Devil, and attacked him. But the laird was well grounded in scripture and kept him at bay with a battery of texts, till at last the Enemy was discomfited and spread his wings to flee, but as a last endeavour ' clechet ' his finger in the by-going, and hooked the laird in the mouth, with the consequence that he and his descendants have had their mouths agley ever since." *(R.C.)*

CLELAND OF THE 1st GENERATION.

ALEXANDER CLELAND (1).—1st Cleland of that ilk. The first of the family of which there is record is Alexander Cleland, or Kneland, of that ilk, in the County of Lanark, who married Margaret, daughter of Adam Wallace of Riccarton, and sistei of Sir Malcolm Wallace, *i.e.*, she was Sir William Wallace's aunt *(Document and Grossart's " History of the Parish of Shotts.")* This Alexander is not mentioned by Nisbet. Probably born about 1230-1240.

CLELANDS OF THE 2nd GENERATION.

JAMES CLELAND (2).—2nd Cleland of that ilk. Probably born between 1260-1270; mentioned 1296-1314. Son and heir of Alexander. "Joined his cousin, Sir William Wallace, in 1296, for the relief of his country against the English, along with the first noblemen and gentlemen of Scotland. He was present at Loudon Hill, July, 1296; at the Battle of Stirling, 13th September, 1297; and at the unfortunate conflict at Falkirk, on Tuesday, 22nd July, 1298, and assisted Sir William Wallace in most of his exploits, particularly in taking prisoner Thomas Longueville, commonly called the 'Red Rover.' After the death of Sir William Wallace he firmly supported the cause of King Robert Bruce, and was present with his eldest son John at the Battle of Bannockburn on Monday, June 24th, 1314, when he was wounded, and for his loyalty and good service the king gave him several lands in the Barony of West Calder in West Lothian. He was succeeded by his eldest son John." *(Document.)*

Grossart adds in addition that he was present at the "skirmish in the High Street of Glasgow in 1300, when Wallace cleft the head of Earl Percy with his sword, and the English were defeated. In 1301 he sailed with Wallace for France, and had a sea-fight with the French pirate, called the 'Red Reiver.'" He further adds that "Cleland is also mentioned in the 'History of the Bruce.' For his loyalty and good service to Robert Bruce he obtained the lands of Calder-clere, now East Calder, in the Barony of Calder, Mid-Lothian."

After the death of Alexander III., James Cleland of Cleland joined with Sir William Wallace against the English for the relief of his country, as in Mr. Blair's "History of Wallace." He afterwards stood firm in his "loyalty for King Robert the Bruce; and for his good service that King gave him several lands lying within the Barony of Calder, in West-Lothian." *(Nisbet's Heraldry 1722.)*

He is frequently mentioned in "Blind Harry's" "Wallace," in which he is twice called cousin to Wallace. Blind Harry's metrical history, however, it must be remembered, was written down many generations (nearly two hundred years) after the events had occurred; still the names and incidents had been kept well in remembrance by being handed down from minstrel to minstrel, and we may consider them substantially correct, though the exploits of the heroes would be much enlarged upon.

The following extracts indicate where "Kneland" is mentioned :—

EXTRACTS FROM "THE METRICAL HISTORY OF SIR WILLIAM WALLACE, KNIGHT OF ELLERSLIE," BY HENRY, COMMONLY CALLED "BLIND HARRY."

Buke thryd.
Line 55
Before the battle of Loudon Hill.

Kneland was thar, ner cusyng to Wallace,
Syne baid with hym in many peralowse place;
And Edward Litill, his sister sone so der
Full weille graithit intill thar armour cler

Line 201.
The Victory.

Litill, Kneland, gert off thair enemyss de,
The Inglissmen tuk playsily part to fle:

Line 330
The Peace.

"Tak pess a quhill, suppose it do ws payne."
So said Adam, the ayr of Rycarttoune
And Kneland als grantyt to thair opynyoun
With thair consent Wallace this pess has tayne
And as his eyme wrocht, till ten moneth war gayne.
Thar leyff thai tuk, with comforde into playn
Santt Jhone to Borche that suld meyt haill agayne.
Boyde and Kneland past to thar placis hayme;

Buke feyrd
Line 137
Banishment
144

And mony othir was full woo that day
. . . And Kneland als, before with him had beyne.
Boid wepyt sor, said; "our leidar is gayne,
"Amang om fays he is set him allayne."
Than Kneland said, "Fals fortoun changis fast,
"Gret God sen we had emir with him past";

Buke sewynd.
249
Before the "Barns of Ayr."

Kerle turnyt with his mastir agayne,
Kneland and Byrd, that mekill war in mayne.

Buke nynte.
Line 32
The Red Rover.

He wyst full weill thai wald nocht all consent
To suffyr him out off the land to go
For thi onon, with outyn wordis mo,
He gart forse, and ordand weill his schip
And thir war part past in his falowschip;
Twa Wallace, was his kymnys men full nar,
Craufurd, Kneland, was heldyn to him der.

Buke nynte.
Line 134

Kneland, cusyng, cum tak the ster on hand;
Her on the waill ner by the I sall stand.
God gyd our schip! as now I say na mar.'

3rd GENERATION.

JOHN CLELAND (3)—3rd of that ilk. Probably born about 1290, mentioned 1314, 1346. Fought with his father at Bannockburn in 1314. Was taken prisoner at the Battle of Durham in October, 1346, with King David II.

4th GENERATION.

No records   Cleland of that ilk probably born about 1330.

5th GENERATION.

No records.   Cleland of that ilk probably born about 1366.

6th GENERATION.

WILLIAM CLELAND (6) —6th Cleland of that ilk. Was probably born about 1390, and not later than 1410. He was one of the witnesses to a charter to the lands of Watston in 1445 from James, Lord Hamilton, to Sir William Baillie of Hoprigg. *(Quoted in Document.)* He is mentioned in reference to his son's marriage in Somerville's "Memorie of the Somervilles." In 1444 "William Cleland of Cleland-toun" is witness to a charter of James Hamilton, Lord of Cadzow (possibly the deed mentioned above). *(Reg. Great Seal of Scotland. Vol. 1424-1513. No. 511.)*

7th GENERATION.

JAMES CLELAND (7) —7th Cleland of that ilk Was probably born about 1420. Married, in 1450, Jean (Janet), youngest daughter of William, 2nd Lord Somerville, by his wife Jean Mowat of Stenhouse.

"Three years thereafter (ι e , in 1450) he (the 2nd Lord Somerville) marryes his youngest daughter Janet upon James Cleilland, sone and heir to William Cleilland of that ilk. The portione is ane thousand and fyve hundred merkes, payable at three termes, and twentieth milk kyne with their followers " *(Somerville's " Memorie of the Somer-villes.")*

Nisbet confuses James, the 7th Cleland, with William, the 6th, for he says :—

"From him (ι e , from James, 2nd Cleland of Cleland) was descended William Cleland of that ilk who in the reign of King James III married Jean, daughter of William Lord Somerville (as in the manuscript of that family) From them branched Cleland of Faskine, Cleland of Monkland and Cleland of Gartness "

PATRICK CLELAND (8) —Sheriff Deputy of Lanarkshire, occurs as a witness in 1457 *(Fraser's Douglas Book)*. He is probably a near relative of this James.

8th GENERATION.

WILLIAM CLELAND (9)—8th Cleland of that ilk. Born about 1451. This generation is omitted by Nisbet and other authorities. Before discovering the name of this man or any reference to him, I had concluded that he existed from the following reasoning: If the Clelands of Faskine, Monkland and Gartness were descended from James Cleland, the 7th of that ilk, and Janet Somerville, there must have been another generation between James, the 7th, and Alexander, since Cleland of Faskine is Alexander's cousin. Moreover, if James Cleland and Janet Somerville were married in 1450, this Alexander, if he is their son and not their grandson, must have been over 60 at the time he was killed at Flodden in 1513—rather too late an age to be participating in an active campaign. Though Nisbet and no other authority mention a generation between these two, I have inserted one, considering such to be warranted by the above statements. Nisbet, indeed, does not state that Alexander was James' son; after discussing James Cleland and Janet Somerville he goes on in a fresh paragraph to state that Alexander Cleland of that ilk was killed at Flodden in 1513, without stating his relationship to the preceding. It is possible, of course, that the Clelands of Faskine, etc., branched off from William Cleland, James' father, and were not offspring of Janet Somerville at all, in which case Alexander, if James' son, would be their cousin. The weight of evidence favours the former view, however.

After forming the opinion that there was a missing generation here, I found mention of it in the "Memorie of the Somervilles." The following are the references, the first one is quoted in full, affording as it does an amusing anecdote* .—

"In Jully 1474, at which tyme the king being disposed to take his pleasure at the poutting in Calder and Carnwath Muires, he acquaints the Lord Somervill with his resolutione, who, by accident was then at court; his majestie being pleased withall to shew him he was resolved for some dayes to be his guest Whereupon the Lord Somervill immediatly dispatches ane expresse to Cowthally (who knew nothing of the king's journey), with a letter to his lady, Dame Marie Baillzie, wherein, according to his ordinary custome when any persones of qualitie wer to be with him, he used to wryte in the postscript of his letters, Speates and Raxes† , and in this letter he had redoubled the

---

* The very curious story which follows must be taken on the authority of tradition The embodying it with so many circumstances was undoubtedly the work of the author himself, who in this, as well as other passages, seems to be ignorant that an affectation of extreme minuteness and precision gives no small cause for suspicion in such cases

† Spits and Ranges ; the latter being the appendage to the kitchen grate, on which the spits turn

same words, because of the extraordinary occasione and worthynes of his guest This letter being delyvered, and the messenger withall telling his lord was very pressing, that it might be speedily and securely put in her ladyship's hands; whereupon she hastily breakes it up, commanding the stewart to read the same, because she could read non herself. This gentleman being but lately entered to his service, and unacquainted with his lord's hand and custome of wrytting, when he comes to the postscript of the letter, he reades Speares and Jacks‡, instead of Speates and Raxes whereupon, my lady all amazed, without considering her husband's ordinary forme of wrytting, falles a weeping supposeing her lord had fallen at vaiiance with some about the court, the king beginning about this tyme to discountenance his ancient nobilitie, and they again to withdraw both ther affectiones and due alleadgeance fiom him. Eftir the reading of the letter, James Inglis of Eistscheill was presently sent for, and commandement given to him and the officers, that all the vassalles, with the able tennents that wer within the two baronies of Carnwath, Cambusnethen, and baillzieiie of Carstaires, should be ready with ther horse and armes to wait upon William Cleilland of that ilk be eight in the morning the ensueing day, and that in order to ther going to Edinburgh This command being punctually obseived by the vassalles and the substantiall tennents§ that wer in use, and obleidged to ryde, by ther holdings and tackes, upon such occasiones, they conveened to the number of two hundred, with the laird of Cleilland, and William Chancellor of Quathquan, with the Baillzie upon ther heads‖ By eleven a clock they wer advanced in ther journey for Edinburgh to the syde of that hill that is somewhat bewest the Corsetthill His majestie haveing breakfasted by nyne in the morning, had taken horse, and was come the lenth of that little watter a myle on this syde of the Corsetthill, bussie, even then, at his sport upon the rode, when the first of all the little company that was with him observed the advance of a troope of men with ther lances, within a myle of him, or thereby. Whereupon all astonished, he calles hastily for the Loid Someivill, who, being at some distance, came upon the spurre. The king being of ane hastie nature, in great fury demanded what the matter meaned, and if he had a mynde to betray him and seize upon his persone the second tyme by ane other treacherous hunting, and withall swearing his head should pay for it if he himself escaped the hands of these traitors, who could be noe other but his vasalles and followers, brought togither off purpose for some ill designe The Lord Someivill, without making any reply, immediately castes himself from his horse to the ground, and falles upon his knees, protesting, with many solemn oaths, that he understood not what the matter meaned, nor what the company

---

‡ Spears and Jacks ; the latter were doublets of leather, quilted with plates of iron, the common armoar of the irregular cavalry of the period.
§ In the last leases of Jedwood forest that were let by the late Duke of Douglas, the tenants were bound to attend him with two well armed hoisemen at least for each farm
‖ *i.e.,* at their head

was, nor the cause of ther being in yonder place, thairfore he humblie begged of his majestie that he would allow him to goe see what they wer, friends or foes; and, for securitie, he had with him his eldest sone and heir William, Barrone of Carnwath; iff all was not weill, and his majestie safe from all hazard, he desyred that his sone's head may be strucken off upon the place. This the king acceptes, and commands him to ryde up and discover what they wer, and the intent of ther being ther; and, according as he found occasione, to returne or give a signe for his reteiring

In the mean tyme, his majestie, with his traine, being about twentieth horse, placed themselves upon the hight of the muir, to marke the Lord Somervill's goeing, and the carriage of the horsemen they beheld, who now made ane halt, when they first observed the king's company, not knowing what they wer, but seeing them draw togither they apprehended they wer noe friends · thairfore they resolved to advance noe further, seeing a horseman comeing up to them with all speed he could make, untill they knew for what intent he came   The Lord Somervill was yet at some distance, when he was presently knoune by severall of the company to be ther lord and master, whereupon the laird of Cleilland, and William Chancellor of Quathquan, galloped out to meet him   He was not a little surprized when he saw them, and demanded the occasione that had brought them togither in that posture and number   To which they answeared, It was by his lordship's directione and his ladye's command   that they wer comeing to Edinburgh to waitt upon him, fearing he had fallen at variance and feud with some one or other about the court.   He desyred to see the letter.   They told him the baillzie had it.   By this tyme they were joyned to the company, where calling for the letter, he made the same to be read, where ther was noe such directione nor orders given as they pretended.   He enquired who read the letter to his lady : they answered his new stewart, who being present, was commanded to read it again, which he did, and comeing to the postscript, reades Speares and Jacks, instead of Speates and Raxes; and herein lay the mistake, that the Lord Somervill knew not whither to laugh or be angry at the fellow   But myndeing the fear he left the king in, and what apprehensiones and jealousies his majestie might intertaine upon his long communing with them, he commanded that they should depart every man to ther respective dwellings; and he himself, with the laird of Cleilland, ans severall other gentlemen, returned to the king, who remained still upon the same place where he had parted from him, unto whom being come he relates the wholl story, whereat the king laughed heartily, calles for a sight of the letter, and reades it himself, swearing it was noe great mistake, for he might have been guiltie of that error himself   His majestie haveing given back the letter, it went from hand to hand amongst these few courtiers that was there, as they proceeded in ther journey, the letter itself containeing noe matter of any consequence but a naked compliment the Lord Somervill had written to his lady.   This is that story of the Speates and Raxes soe much discoursed of then, as it is to this day amongst persons of qualité; for of late the Duke of Lauderdale, when he was commissioner, at a full table of the greatest part of the nobilitie in Scotland, then dyneing with him, related the wholl story allmost in the same termes that I have set it doune" *(Vol I pp 240-247)*

This William Cleland is again mentioned in p. 297, when King James IV., in 1489, and the second year of his reign, is received by the Somervilles near Inglestoune Bridge, when he comes to the marriage entertainment given by the Lord Somerville at the nuptials of his son with the half-sister of Archibald Bell-the-Cat.

"John Lord Somervill, by reasone of his age was not able to meet the king at any distance However, being supported by William Somervill, younger of Plaine, and William Cleilland of that ilk, both his nephewes, he receaved the king at the west end of the calsay that leades from Carnwath toune to Cowthally house."

It was this John Lord Somerville's sister who married James Cleland, 7th of that ilk, so William Cleland being called his nephew proves conclusively the existence of this the 8th generation and the name of the chief.

Another reference to this William Cleland is found in the "Laing Charters," where on 8th April, 1478, a "precept of Clare Constat" is addressed to him and others.

RODGER CLEILLAND (10) —This individual is mentioned in 1489 as being a witness to a proclamation by James Lord Hamilton. *("Memorie of the Somervilles," p. 301.)* He may have been a brother of William Cleland, 8th of that ilk.

9th GENERATION.

ALEXANDER CLELAND (11).—9th Cleland of that ilk. "Of that ilk" in 1498. Killed at Flodden in 1513

"Alexander Cleland of that ilk with his cousin William Cleland of Faskine, were both killed fighting valiantly for their king in the fatal battle of Flowden 1513. I have seen the seal of arms of this Alexander, appended to a Charter of the date 1498, upon which was an Hare saliant, with an Hunting-Horn about his neck." *(Nisbet's Heraldry, 1722)*

10th GENERATION.

JAMES CLELAND (12).—10th Cleland of that ilk Married a daughter of Hepburn of Bonnytown, son of Patrick Lord Hailes, Earl of Bothwell. Died 1547.

"James Cleland of that ilk, an eminent man in the time of King James V. whom he frequently attended while hunting, as in the above-mentioned manuscript, married a daughter of Hepburn of Bonnytown, descended of the Earl of Bothwell, by whom he had his son and successor Alexander " *(Nisbet)*

James Cleland, or Kneland "de eodem," appears as witness several times in 1511 and 1543. *(Reg Great Seal.)* His sons were Alexander, Arthur (first Cleland of Known-noblehill), Roben (Robert), and John. He had one daughter at least, Janet, whose marriage contract was drawn up in 1536. He made his will and testament in July, 1547, and died shortly afterwards. The following simple recital has an interest far above its mere genealogical value :—

"Testamentum Quond Jacobi Kneland de eod. Inventarium arn^m bonorum quond Jacobi Kneland de eod. factum per os decendentis, apud Knelandtine, duodecio. die mens. July, Anno Dni. Jaj V^o XLVII etc.

Duodecimo die mensis July.

Memorandum. That I James Kneland of that ilk ordanes my testament in pis manere, That is to say, I leyf and ordains my executouris, my wife and my eldest son, Alex^r I leyff and ordains pt my eldest sone, Sanderis, haif my heritage and my airschip, as efferis . Alsua, I ordane & makis my son Arthure assigney in and to my stedying of Knokhobohill; And gif it failyesis of Arthure, as God forbid, I ordane my son Robene to have pe said stedying of Knokhobohill : Alsua, I ordane pt my eldest son, Sander^{is} pt he pay thankfully to my son Johne, yeirlye, pe sume of X lib of pis realme, ay and quhill he geif and resign pe Clerkschip of pe east kirk of Caldercleir to my son John. He doand pis, I will pt he be dischargit of pe X lib foirsaid *Item,* I ordane, gif any of my sonnis, Arthure, Robert or Johne, sleip or deas, pt ay ane succied to ane vp^r as efferis, or quhay pt misteris maist, as may be knawyn be pair moder.　 . . *Item,* I ordane pt my obsequeis be done honestlye in pe kirk of Bothwell, and ane honest orbit , and pat my executouris (sub) sest and preyst for ane yeir, to syng mass for my saule : And ordanes my wife ilk yeir to caus ane saul mas and dirige to be done for me about pe samyn day twelmont pat it sall happin me to deces " etc Confirm die XXII mes. Mtij. Anno. Dni Jaj. V^c XLVII. *(" Commissary Records Glasgow," as quoted by Hamilton of Wishaw.)*

In the "Memorie of the Somervilles" the "Laird of Cleilland" is mentioned in 1517 as being one of the gentlemen assembled to pay honour to Hugh Lord Somerville's second wife, Lady Janet Maitlane, when he brings her home to Carnwath. This Cleland of that ilk must be James the 10th of that ilk. In a deed about 1541, James Wood of Brymslie appears to be his ward. *(Reg. Great Seal.)*

ELIZABETH CIELAND (13), of the 10th generation, daughter of Alexander, 9th Cleland of Cleland, married John

Robertson of Earnock, son of Robert Robertson and Margaret, daughter of John Hamilton of Terrance. *(Document)*

11th GENERATION.

ALEXANDER CLELAND (14).—11th Cleland of that ilk. (Chief 1547-159 ?.) Son of James, 10th Cleland of Cleland; married a daughter of Hamilton of Haggs. Mentioned in 1565. He at least was alive in 1572, since Wm. Cleland, younger, of Cleland (evidently his son) is mentioned at that date by the title " younger." Grossart says he died near the beginning of the 17th Century.

"Alexander Cleland of that ilk, eminent for his loyalty on behalf of Queen Mary: he married Margaret, a daughter of Hamilton of Haggs by whom he had William his son and successor." *(Nisbet, 1722)*

"Haggs is now Rosehall. He was one of those summoned to appear before Parliament the 12th March 1565, to see and hear the doom of forfaltour ordourly led against them for the crimes committit be them content in said summons." *(Grossart's " History of the Parish of Shotts," 1880)*

ARTHUR CLELAND (15).—1st Cleland of Knowenoblehill. Married Margaret Pollart   Alexander's brother. Given the patrimony of Knowenoblehill by his father's, James', will, 1547. Mentioned in 1572 as being guilty art and part in the murders of Darnley and the two Regents. Founder of the branch of Clelands of Knowenoblehill   In 1559 a charter is granted to him and his wife of some lands, in which Alexander Cleland of that ilk and William Cleland (probably Alexander's son) are mentioned. *(Renwick's Glasgow Protocols.)* Mentioned in 1572   *(Reg Privy Council)*

ROBEN (ROBERT) CLELAND (16).—Son of James, 10th Cleland. No mention except in the will.

ANDREW CLELAND (17), patruus (paternal uncle) of William Cleland, 12th of that ilk, servitor of D Rich Maitland of Lithingtoun, notary, writer, &c., appears frequently as a witness between 1569 and 1612. He was a writer in Edinburgh John Cleland, his brother germane, is mentioned with him, in 1588, together with Elizabeth Kneland, wife of William Cuthberton in Ledoun *(Reg. Great Seal)*. He also appears as procurator several times about 1600 in the Privy Council Register. In 1612 Andrew Cleland, one of the baillies of Edinburgh, is granted sasine. His seal is a " hare or rabbit rampant with a hunting horn," etc. *(Scotch Seals.)*

JOHN CLELAND (18), son of James, 10th Cleland. Prob-

ably the John Cleland who is witness to the marriage contract of Janet Cleland, daughter of James, 10th Cleland, in
1536 In 1588 mentioned as being Andrew Cleland's brother,
as above. John Cleland, notary, is a witness between the
years 1585-1599. *(Reg Privy Council.)*

ELIZABETH KNELAND (19), mentioned above as the wife of
William Cuthberton, is perhaps a sister of John and Andrew,
since the three names occur in connection with a charter to
her and her husband.

JANET CLELAND (20), daughter of James Cleland, 10th of
that ilk. The marriage contract between her and William
Dalmahoy was drawn up in 1536 and, as it is an interesting
document and one illustrative of the manners of the time, its
text is here reproduced

"Apud Striveling 16 Jul Rex confirmavit cartam Alexandri
Dalmahoy de eodem,—(qua,—pro perimpletione contractus inter se et
Jacobum Cleland de eodem initi penes matrimonium inter personas
subscriptas,—Concessit Jonete Cleland filie dicti Jac , in ejus pura
virginitate, in vitali redditu, et filio suo et heredi apparenti Willelmo
Dalmahoy in feodo, et heredibus inter ipsum et dictam Jon legitime
procreandis, quibus deficientibus, legitimis et propinquioribus heredibus
dicti Wil quibuscumque,—10 bovatas terrarum (viz., unam per Kenti-
gernum Patersone, 3 per Joh Winram juniorem, 2 per Alex. Aliss-
chender, 2 per Johannem Winram seniorem, 2 per Joh Thomsoun
occupatas) in villa de Dalmahoy, ac occidentalem quartam partem
terrarum dominicalium de D (prebentem annuatim celdram ordei et
celdram farine avenatice), vic. Edinburgh —Tenend. de regi .—Test.
    . .   Joh Cleland .   —Apud Edinburgh. 10 Jul. 1536
(Reg Great Seal.)

12th GENERATION.

WILLIAM CLELAND (21).—12th Cleland of that ilk. Chief
about 1597 (?). William, the son and successor of Alexander,
married the sister (Elizabeth (?) or Marion) of Walter Stewart,
the first Lord Blantyre. *(Nisbet)* His wife Elizabeth was a
daughter of Sir John Stewart of Minto by his wife Margaret,
daughter of James Stewart of Cardonald. *(Document)*
Mentioned, apparently as the heir, in 1565, 1572. As Chief
in 1600, 1601. In 1572 charged with being guilty art and
part in the murders of Darnley and the two Regents.
William Cleland of Cleland, with his brothers, Arthur and
John, and John Cleland in Foscane, Gavin Cleland in Glenhuif, James Robertson of Ernouk (William Cleland's cousin),
and many others, are mentioned in the "Remission to the
Duke of Chatelherault and others, 1565," thus .-

" Henry and Mary, King and Queen of Scotland, &c   Because
from our special grace and favour we remit to our well-beloved, our
dearest cousin, James, Duke of Chatelherault, Earl of Arran and
Lord Hamilton, John, David and Claud Hamilton his sons, Gavin,
Commendator of Kilwinning, with the remaining persons of the name,
and others, retainers and vassals of the ancient house of the said Duke,
with the tenants, occupiers of, and inhabitants upon his and their
lands, in special and general as follows."—Here follows a long list of
the names, after which it proceeds —" Also to all other holders and
occupiers of lands belonging to the said Lord Duke, and other persons
aforesaid, living within our Kingdom of Scotland   And to all retainers
and Dependents of the ancient house of the said Lord Duke, in general,
we remit our Royal displeasure, and every charge which we have had,
now have, or can have, in any way, on account of the treasonable
detention of the Castles of Hamilton and Draffen, lying within our
county of Lanark, and that, after our mandate had been issued by our
officers, in virtue of our letters to affect this our order, in so far as that
they should deliver up these Castles to us, and to our officers appointed
in our name.   And for all other charges of treason, as well not named
as named, or whatever weight or importance ; and for all other charges
in general.   Also for all other indictments and charges which may
follow thereupon, or which may be imputed either to the said persons
specially or generally, or to any one of them, (treasonable attempts
upon our person, wilful fire-raising, murder, &c , only excepted), &c ,
&c   At Edinburgh, this second day of January, one thousand five
hundred and sixty years, and of our reigns the first and twenty-
fourth "

Evidently William Cleland's father, Alexander, did not
participate in this remission, since three months later, in
March, we find him appearing before Parliament to hear the
" doom of forfaltour led against him," as previously
mentioned.

" July 28th, 1572 —Arthur Cleland of Knowenoblehill and William
Cleland, younger, of Cleland, were charged with being guilty, art and
part, in the murders of Darnley and the two Regents, and had to find
security for their appearance at the next ' Justice-air ' at Lanark, upon
fifteen day's warning   Cleland of Cleland became security for Arthur
Cleland in 500 merks, and Dalmahoy for William Cleland, younger, in
2,000 pounds "   *(Grossart)*

In 1572 William Cleland of that ilk is pledge and surety
(Reg. Privy Council)   In 1579, Math. Stewart, younger, of
Mynto, is caution for William Kneland of that ilk, that he
will not abet the two rebel Hamiltons. *(Reg Privy Council.)*
In 1590, the Cleland of Cleland. probably this William, is
mentioned in a list of "landit men"—a list probably

intended for the guidance of Chancellor Maitland's Government in matters of taxation   *(Idem.)*

This William Cleland of that ilk is mentioned again in 1600. On June 1st, 1601, "William Cleilland of that ilk" appears as a witness to a document of the Earl of Marre's. *("Memorie of the Somerville's," Vol 11, p 66)*

In 1603, James Tennent of Tenhous is surety for William Cleland of that ilk, not to harm James Libertoun in Nether Libertoun, in the sum of 1,000 merks; and William Cleland of that ilk is surety in 300 merks for James Cleland, son of William Cleland in Ormiston hill, and James Tennant of Tinhous, for Robert Kneland of Farmylne, to the same effect. Again in the same year he is surety for James, Andro, Claud, John, and Archibald, his sons; for James Cleland, son of William Cleland of Ormiston hill, for Robert Kneland in Fairmylne, and John Cleland, his son, to the same effect.

William Cleland is said to have been one of 50 gentlemen who met Queen Mary when she escaped from Loch Leven. *(R.C.)*

The will of "William Cleland of that ilk, par. of Calder-Clcire, regality of Dalkeith, Sher. of Edinburgh," is confirmed, 20th June, 1608   *(Commiss. of Edin.)*

ARTHUR CLELAND (22), his brother.

JOHN CLELAND (23), his brother.

WILLIAM CLELAND (24), of Ormistonhill, and JAMES (25), his son; ROBERT KNELAND (26), of Fairmylne, and JOHN (27), his son, are evidently, from the above, near relatives of William Cleland, 12th of that ilk.

JANET CLELAND (28), spouse of William Grenschelis of that ilk, is probably a near relative of William Cleland of that ilk, since in 1589 we find his signature, that of William Cleland of Knowhobilhill, and that of John Cleland, Notary, to a sale of land by her and her husband *(Glasgow Protocols)*

13th GENERATION.

(a) JAMES CLELAND (29) —13th Cleland of that ilk. Succeeded, 1608; died probably about 1635. Since William Cleland, the preceding, was evidently at man's estate in 1565 and again in 1572, we may suppose him to have been about 30 at the latter date, if not several years older. In 1608, when he died, he must have been over 60 at least. It is obviously impossible that this James was his brother (as Grossart suggests) In fact, we have mention of Arthur and John as being his brothers, but no mention of a James. More-

over, this James was alive in or about 1634, and it is
inconceivable that, inheriting his title in 1601, when his
brother was about 60, he himself being not much less, he
retained it for 34 years longer. Evidently this James is the
son of the preceding William, which would account for his
signing himself, or being styled, James Cleland of Cleland in
1590, before his predecessor's death.

He escapes Nisbet's notice altogether, who states that
James' son, Alexander, was the son (it should be grandson) of
William, the 12th of that ilk. The "Document" before-
mentioned mixes up William the 12th and James the 13th
thus :—" William, 11th Cleland of that ilk, married first a
sister of Walter Stewart, etc, by whom he had his son and
successor Alexander. He married secondly Mary Somerville,
daughter of Sir James Somerville, etc., and had issue by
her." Now we know by the following that it was James, 13th
Cleland of Cleland, who married this Mary Somerville, and
not William the 12th. In the "Memorie of the Somervilles,"
in speaking of James, fourth Baron of Cambusnethan, called
"Velvet Eye," it says : "for his daughters they were two
. . . the second, named Mary, was marryed upon James
Cleilland of that ilk, of ane anciente house and familie as is
in Cleddesdale. . . . . For his other sone-in-law, the
Laird of Cleilland, albeit he had been at much paines and
expenses to keep up that house. yet at his death it was but
in a staggering condition." This daughter is referred to
later on in the same work as "Lady Cleilland," thus : "ten
thousand merks debt which he had contracted for paying the
tochers of his two daughters, the Lady Somervill and the
Lady Cleilland."

We find this James styled "of that ilk" in a test, dated
1590 and confirmed in 1606. "James Cleland of that ilk
occurs February, 1590. Test. Wylie, in Bothwell-Scheillis,
Conf October, 18, 1606."—Commis. Rec. Glasg., quoted by
Hamilton. Whether he is styled "of that ilk" in 1590, when
his father William was alive, or whether the "of that ilk"
is added when the will is confirmed in 1606, when his father
was dead, does not appear He may have been called "of
that ilk" while his father was alive, though old, since he was
the heir.

James Cleland of that ilk appears in the Test. of Helen
Finlay, spouse to Thomas Dougall in Nether Dunsistoun (in
Bartrum Shottis), "Quha deceist in pe moneth of March or
p^r by 1609," conf. September 10, 1610 ; and James Somerville,
elder, of Cambusnethan, who deceased September. 1623, leaves

legacies to "Jeane and Mareoune Clelandis, his oyes (*i.e.*, grandchildren), dochers to James Cleland of that ilk," conf. January 2nd, 1624 "Waltir Cleland, brother germane to James Cleland of that ilk," appears as cautioner in the test of Stewart of Christiswoll. Conf. October 3rd, 1633. Commiss. Rec. Glasg., quoted by Hamilton of Wishaw.

In September, 1621, "James Cleland of that ilk" "the laird of Cleland," signs a bond borrowing 100 merks from James Wilson, elder, burgess of Hamilton; in November, 1621, he signs another bond acknowledging a debt of "thirteen score pounds" (Scots), to John Gilmour, merchant, burgess of Glasgow, and his brother Claud is a witness to it; in 1626 he signs a similar bond, borrowing 109 merks 5 shillings and 8 pennies (Scots), which is witnessed by Alex Cleland, younger, of that ilk; Claud Clelland, his brother; and James Clelland, his son. (*Comm. Rec. Glasg.*)

(*b*) WALTER CLELAND (30), above mentioned. Probably the Walter Cleland, servitor to the Laird of Blakhill, "assignay constitut be Alexander Hunter in Bottohburne," 1636. (*Com. Rec. Glasg.*)

(*c*) ANDRO CLELAND (31), son of Wm. Cleland of that ilk. James Cleland of that ilk, and Andrew, his brother, are witnesses, 1627. (*Laing Charters*) He is a witness again in 1641. (*Reg Great Seal*) (See 12th Gen)

(*d*) CLAUD CLELAND (32).—(Ditto). This Claud is probably the pupil of Glasgow College mentioned in 1598. He appears as a witness to a deed signed by his brother James of that ilk, in 1626.

(*e*) JOHN CLELAND (33).—(See above.)

(*f*) ARCHIBALD CLELAND (34)—(Ditto). James Dunlop of that ilk in 1609 is surety for Elizabeth Stewart, Lady Kneland, in 100 merks, and for Andro Archibald and Johne Knelandis, brothers of the Laird of Kneland, 500 merks each, not to harm David Little of Badronisgill, or Thomas Anderson, his servant. (*Reg. Privy Council.*)

(*g*) ALEXANDER CLELAND (35), brother germane to James Cleland of that ilk, in 1630 signs a bond. (*Comm Rec. Glasg*)

14th GENERATION.

(*a*) ALEXANDER CLELAND (36), heir (?14th) of that ilk. Eldest son of James Cleland, 13th of that ilk. Married about 1620 the sister of John Hamilton, first Lord Bargeny (*Douglas' "Baronage," Anderson's "History of the Hamiltons"*) Their son and heir sold the lands of Cleland to a cousin of his own

name. *(Nisbet, 1722.)* Nisbet refers to this man as being
the eldest son of William Cleland and of his wife, the sister of
Walter Stewart, but Nisbet has missed a generation (as Grossart points out), and Alexander is not the son but the grandson of William Cleland

> About 1620 " Alexander . .   married Mary, sister of John
> Hamilton, first Lord Bargany, and youngest son of Sir John Hamilton
> of Bargany, and his spouse, Margaret Campbell, daughter of the Rev.
> Alexander Campbell,—Bishop of Brechin—of Ardkinglas descended
> from Argyle; by her he had several sons, the eldest of whom sold the
> lands of Cleland to a cousin of his own name " *(" History of the
> Hamiltons " Document.)*

In 1626, Alexander Cleland, younger, of that ilk, together with his brother James and uncle Claud Cleland, are
witnesses to a deed signed by James Cleland of that ilk.
(Comm. Rec. Glasg.)

In 1632, " Alexander Cleland of that ilk " contributes 20
merks to the fund " for building of a common librarie within
the Colledge of Glasgow," etc. Charles R. gives £200 sterling
for the same purpose; "James, Marqueis of Hamilton,
Earle of Arran and Cambridge, ane thousand merks Scottish
money "; and many others contribute. Claud Clelland, who
in 1598 is a student there, is probably his uncle, and hence
his interest in the College. *(Munim Univ Glasguen)*

A controversy has recently taken place over the marriage of this
man and as to whether he ever was " Cleland of that ilk," or died
merely the heir The following quotation of Hamilton of Wishaw
from the Commiss Rec Glasg throws light on the subject ·—
" Alexander Cleland, fear (i e , heir) of that ilk . decisit in the
monthe of July, 1634." His testament in which " Wm Cleland,
brother of ye defunct " is mentioned is confirmed Nov. 5th following;
and " Andro and Ard. Clelandis, brother-germane to the defunct, are
afterwards served to him, and confirmed June 16, 1643 " From this it
would appear that this Alexander of the 14th generation died in 1634,
while heir of that ilk, and before his father's death So that he
himself was never (14th) Cleland of that ilk, but his son, who sold the
lands to his cousin, was. I think it probable that this son was left
a mere child at his father's death, that when his grandfather of that
ilk died he was left in the custody of his uncle James, second son to
James, 13th of that ilk, and younger brother to Alexander, that this
James induced the boy to sell to him or to his eldest son the family
estate for ready money—a thing a boy would be very likely to do;
that some while after this was done, this James, living, as he naturally
would after his father's death and during the minority of his nephew,
in Cleland House, assumed (wrongfully) the title of Cleland of that

ilk   He would be naturally spoken of by his neighbours before this as Cleland of Cleland House, or even of Cleland, so the assumption of the title would be easy and unlikely to be much questioned by his young nephew, who was probably somewhat ashamed of having sold his birthright   This hypothesis accounts rationally for the sale of the property, a thing that a grown-up chief of a family would be very unlikely to do unless he were sorely in debt or some cogent reason required it, it is much more feasible to suppose that the uncle allured his young nephew with gold.   Likewise by this means we can account for the traditional indignation of the descendants in the direct line at a younger branch carrying the principal arms of the family, and for the incident where one of them, probably the Cleland of that ilk of the 18th generation, deletes the supporters from a coat-of-arms on a carriage in Prince's St., Edinburgh, with a painter's brush seized from a passing tradesman.   Perhaps this James Cleland thought that, having bought the property, he had bought the name too, but as the " Herald and Genealogist " for December, 1867, points out, this is incorrect, and a family though deprived of their possession are still entitled to be called by its name

The Rose-Clelands of Rath-Gael, Co Down, claim to be descended from this Alexander of the 12th generation, through John, his second or third son, who was born about 1623   Probably then, his elder brother, who sold the estates, was born about 1620, and would be only 14 years old when his father died   Since the last mention of James Cleland, 13th of that ilk, is in 1633, he probably died not very much later, so that the conjecture as to the youth of this son of Alexander when he became Cleland of that ilk is well supported.   The Rose-Cleland's genealogy goes on to say, " in consequence of some disagreement with his elder brother he retired in disgust to a small property called ' Laird Braes ' in Co of Wigton." I think this disagreement probably arose over the sale of the property mentioned above, and that his brother John was given " Laird Braes " at this time, while he himself retained one or two small properties (perhaps Mouse-Mill near Lanark, said to be the last property in the neighbourhood owned by the main branch), where John Cleland W.S , 19th Cleland of that ilk, probably died in 1777.

The claim of these Rose-Clelands to descent from Alexander Cleland of the 12th generation is combated by a writer in the " Herald and Genealogist " for December, 1867. The following are his arguments, which, since they might also be used against the main stem of the family, I insert —

" But unluckily for the house of Rath-Gael, it happens that its patriarch, *the sole connecting link with* these personages, ' Alexander Cleland, fear (i e , heir apparent), ' of that ilk, deceist in the monethe of July, 1634, *in the lifetime of his father, James* (not William, as in the pedigree), *and unmarried,* as is proved by his testament, confirmed by the Commissary of Glasgow on 5th November thereafter, and sub juer(dat   \ h u his tinee younger brothers take up his

personal succession His second brother, James, succeeded his father
in the estate, and is found, so late as 1656, styled ' of that ilk,' formerly ' second lawfull sone to umqll James Cleland of that ilk,' in
another deed in these same records " *(Com Rec. Glasg)*

Now, this writer's quotations are not taken direct, as he would lead
one to suppose, from the " Commiss Records of Glasgow," but from
notes in Hamilton of Wishaw's " Sheriffdoms of Lanark and Renfrew,"
compiled in 1710. Moreover he does not quote correctly, leaving out
a . . .   between " fear of that ilk " and decisit in the monethe "
which occurs in Hamilton Moreover, in Hamilton there is no mention
of Alexander being unmarried, and no word about his three younger
brothers taking up the *personal* succession, although it does say that
" Andro & Ard Clelandis, brether germane to the defunct, are afterwards served to him " We have in fact definite statements in other
places that he was married, of his wife's name, and of his children
It is true, Alexander may never have come into possession of the
Cleland Estates, but his son did · and, alas, sold them

The critic of the Rose-Cleland's genealogy goes on to say :—" The
story of the sale is a pure fiction, for the main stem retained their
estate till the beginning of the eighteenth century. William Hamilton
of Wishaw, a local antiquary of some repute, and a neighbouring laird,
whose estate closely adjoined that of Cleland, and who flourished in
the latter half of the 17th century, thus notices the head of the family
in his ' Description of the Sheriffdom of Lanark,' compiled before
1710 He calls the Laird of Cleland ' very old (*i e*, the family), and
the chief of that name ' (p. 40) Now, had the laird of his day been
merely the representative of the ' cousin of his own name ' who, as we
are desired to believe by this pedigree, purchased the estate from a
man who never existed (the *eldest* son of the *childless* Alexander),
Wishaw, who was thoroughly acquainted with all the surrounding
families, would not have called him the ' chief ' It is well known in
Scotland that the chief of a family retains his style ' of that ilk,'
although the lands have left his possession. And, by Scottish usage,
the 'owner merely by *purchase* of an estate bearing his name would
never be honoured with the dignity of ' that ilk.' "

As arguments against the above conclusions, note :—

(1) Though in 1710 the " Laird of Cleland " is called Chief of that
name he is not styled " Cleland of that ilk "   there would be less com-
punction, if in doubt, in calling a man " chief of the name " than in
calling him " of that ilk "

(2) That this very Hamilton of Wishaw's daughter was married to
the " Laird of Cleland "; for Grossart in 1880 says : " In 1685 and
also in 1689 Alexander Cleland of Cleland was one of the Commissioners of Supply, and married Margaret Hamilton, daughter of William
Hamilton of Wishaw, about 1680 "

(Note—Exception is taken to this Alexander being styled Cleland
of Cleland, inasmuch as he is a descendant of the " cousin of the
same name " whose family assumed the title " of that ilk.")

John Cleland, F.R S , in a note says of this : " Perhaps the very circumstance of his being an antiquary tempted him to the dishonesty of calling him 'chief.'" He then goes on to point out that the sale is mentioned in " Nisbet," that " Nisbet " says Major Wm. Cleland, Commissioner of Customs, great-grandson of the Alexander whose son sold the estates, was the head in 1722 : that in 1880, the Clelands (his branches) all acknowledged John Fullarton Cleland of Australia as the head of the family (through the Commissioner) ; and he reverts to the story of the brushing out of the supporters in Princes St

(3) That in 1710 Hamilton of Wishaw mentions Cleland House as the seat of " the Laird of Cleland," but in 1722 Wm. Hamilton, incumbent of Bothwell Parish, in speaking of the same place says that it was " antiently the seat of the Clelands of that ilk " Surely if the estate had only recently left the hands of the Clelands of that ilk he would have put it " until recently," or even given the date Instead he says "antiently," which signifies a period measured by many years Does Hamilton of Wishaw, by saying " the seat of the Laird of Cleland, very old and chief of that name," mean that this *had been* the *chief seat* of the *very old* family of that name, viz , the Lairds of Cleland? Since the " very old " refers to the family (as the critic in the " Genealogist " informs us) why may not the " chief of that name " also do so, and indicate merely that this was at one time the chief seat of the Clelands of Cleland from which they derived their name?

I think it may be stated that the claims of the Rose-Clelands to descent from the second son, John, of Alexander Cleland, heir of that ilk of the 14th generation, are in no way invalidated by this attack of the writer in the " Genealogist," whose conclusions are shown to be erroneous

JAMES CLELAND (37), the " usurper," 2nd son of James, 13th of that ilk, after the death of his brother Alexander in 1634, and during the minority of his nephew, assumed the title " of that ilk." He apparently finally persuaded his nephew to sell to him, or to his son Alexander, the estates of Cleland It is a noteworthy point that in 1672 " James Cleland of that ilk " recorded the usual arms of the Clelands of that ilk in the Lyon Register, but *without supporters*, while in 1717 Major William Cleland, " lineal representative of the family of Cleland of that ilk," registers them *with the supporters*, he being a great-grandson of this James' brother, Alexander.

In 1626, James Cleland, son of James of that ilk, appears as a witness to his father's bond.

About 1649 we find the Laird of Cleland (probably James, brother of Alexander of the 14th Generation, and second son of James, 13th of that ilk) mentioned in the " Me moir of the S merville," C r n (u th n (James Somer-

ville of Drum, grandson of Hugh, Lord Somerville), in spite
of an Act passed by the General Assembly at the time (afterwards rescinded), resolved to bury his eldest daughter in the
Choir of Cambusnethan Kirk. They wrote a letter to him,
but he " was fully determined to bury his daughter within the
quier, which the Lairds of Raplock, Cleilland, and Millburne,
with others of his relations, being informed off, they came to
Camnethan, and dealt very earnestly with him not to break
the Act of the Assemblie," etc., which induced him to relin-
quish his purpose and bury her without the church.

In 1651 " James Cleilland of that ilke," together with
Gavin Hamilton of Raploch and Robert Hamilton of Millburne, accompany Cambusnethan and his son to " Corsefoord
boat, a passage upon Clyde," to treat with Corhouse and his
friends about the mairiage settlements, etc., of the latter's
daughter with Cambusnethan the younger; the pair being
married two months later, November, 1651, in Lesmahago
Church.

In 1654, " Cambusnethan efter his returne, having
visited his relations Raploch, Cleilland, and Millburne, these
three gentlemen being cautioners for most of his debts," they
give him some advice about the settlement of these.

Grossart says " the last notice of James is in the testament of John Hamilton, burgess in Hamilton, who died in
1656, where he is styled James Cleland of that ilk, second son
of the deceased James Cleland of that ilk How long James
Cleland survived the above date I am not informed, but he
was succeeded by his son Alexander, who was the last of the
Clelands of Cleland." It has already been pointed out that
he was not the last Cleland of Cleland, but the last of the
younger branch who assumed that title.

In the test of " Johne Hamiltone, falconer, burges of Hamiltone,"
who deceased October, 1656, the following item occurs .—Award ' be
James Cleland, now of pt ilk, be band, pn designit second lawll sone
to umqll James Cleland of that ilk & his caris be twa bands, Vjc '
(xxxiii. li Conf. October 16, 1657 *Com. Rec. Glasg*)

In 1655 " James Cleland of Cleland townmylne," enters into a bond
for himself and " Jounet Stirling his spouse relict to umqll Johne
Aittoun at Cleland tounmylne, her first husband." *(Comm Rec
Glasg)* This James Cleland is possibly James Cleland self-styled of
that ilk, since Cleland Mill lay very close to Cleland House

JAMES CLELAND, " of Cleland," is on a Committee of
war for Lanark (1644), on a committee for revaluing Lanark
(1647), on a Committee of War (1648), a Commissioner of

Excise (1661), a Justice of the Peace (1663), and a Commissioner of Supply (1667, 1678, 1685). *(Thomson's Acts.)*

(c) WILLIAM CLELAND (38), brother of Alexander, mentioned above.

(d) ANDREW CLELAND (39), brother of Alexander, mentioned above.

"And Cleland, fratre germano *Joannis C. de Eodem* is a witness to a Charter of D Joanni Hamilton de Barganie to D Joanni Hamiltoun de Carridin and his wife Lady Jean Douglas, 22 July, 1632 " *(Conf. 9 March, 1638. Reg Great Seal.)*

(e) This JOHN CLELAND (40) of Cleland, must be another brother of Alexander; the application of " de eodem " to him shows the loose way in which the term was applied at this time, when his brother James styled himself Cleland of Cleland too, though his nephew, the son of Alexander, was the real Cleland of that ilk, though a child.

(f) ARTHUR CLELAND (41), brother of Alexander, mentioned above

(g) JEAN CLELAND (42), daughter of James Cleland, grandchild of James Somerville, elder, of Cambusnethan. Mentioned in a legacy, 1624.

(h) MARIAN CLELAND (43), ditto.

15th GENERATION.

——— CLELAND (44).—15th Cleland of Cleland, son of Alexander Cleland, of the 14th Generation, heir of that ilk. Born about 1621 "Sold the lands of Cleland to a cousin of his own name." *(Nisbet.)*

JOHN CLELAND (45).—Second or third son of Alexander Cleland of the 14th Generation, of Laird Braes, in the Parish of Laswalt, County of Wigton Born about 1623 Owing to some disagreement with his elder brother he retired in disgust to Laird Braes. Married about 1651 Katherine Ross, died in 1683, leaving his son and successor, James Cleland, of Laird Braes, said to be the ancestor of the Clelands of Rath-Gael, County Down, Ireland

ALEXANDER CLELAND (46).—Son of James Cleland the younger, brother to Alexander of the 14th Generation. Self-styled " Cleland of Cleland," and owner of Cleland Estate. This is probably the Alexander Cleland, "pupil of the 4th Class," in Glasgow College, in 1675. Grossart says of him ·—

" In 1685 and also in 1689, Alexander Cleland of Cleland was one of the Commissioners of Supply He was married to Margaret Hamilton, daughter of William Hamilton of Wishaw. This marriage

must have taken place about 1680, as William Hamilton of Wishaw
was married in 1660, and could not have a marriageable daughter much
earlier than that date   The following curious corroborative document
is here introduced for preservation ·—

Edinr., Dec. 2nd, 1726

" Pay to me, Margaret Hamilton, relict of the deceast Alexander
Cleland of that ilk, or order at Muirhead's Coffee House in Edinburgh,
betwixt and the tenth day of January next, nyne pounds four shillings
and eleven pence halfpennie sterl., value received by you of me.

" Margaret Hamilton."

" To Gavin Hamilton,

Purchaser of the estate of Cleland "

" Accepts—Gavin Hamilton "

Margaret Hamilton, or Lady Cleland as she was then called, was
life-rented in part of Cleland estate, and long survived her husband,
which may explain her connection with Gavin Hamilton at the above
date.

Alexander, as I have already stated, was the last of the Clelands
of Cleland. Finding himself deeply indebted to William Hamilton of
Wishaw, Archibald Hamilton of Dalserf, advocate, and many other
persons, he sold and disponed Cleland estate, in 1702, to William and
Archibald Hamilton, for behoof of his creditors, and shortly after his
death, or in 1711, it was sold by public roup, and purchased by Gavin
Hamilton of Inverdovat for the sum of £29,185 5s 8d Scots money,
being £2,432 sterling

At the date of sale the estate is described as—" All and Haill the
lands of Clelandtoun, called the five pund land of Clelandtoun with
the tower and fortalice, &c —in the barony of Bothwell—All and Haill
the fortie shilling land of Little Hareshaw, in the parish of Shotts—
All and Haill the lands of Newarthill and Whitagreen—All and Haill
the Mains and Mill of Carphin—Excepting therefra the feu ferm
rights of Little Hareshaw " The teinds, both vicarage and parsonage,
of the lands of Blairmucks, in Shotts parish, were sold with Cleland
estate. Alexander Inglis Hamilton, of Murdoston, sold Cleland estate
in 1766, to Captain Hew Dalrymple, of Fordal, for £6,310 sterling

Alexander Cleland of Clelandtoun is a Commissioner for
the Militia and also of Supply (1689) *(Thomson's Acts)*
"Cleland of that ilk," collector of cess, 1701.

MARGARET CLELAND (47).—Daughter of Cleland of that
ilk (probably James, brother of Alexander).   Married John
Hamilton, 10th of Udston, Sheriff of Lanarkshire.   They had
a son, John, and a daughter Margaret, married to Hamilton
of Barr. *(Hist. of the Hamiltons)*

16th GENERATION.

———— CLELAND (48) —Grandson of Alexander, 14th Cleland, and father of Major William Cleland, Commissioner of Customs.

"JACOBUS CLELAND (49) —D. Cleland de eodem hœres, pupil of the 4th Class, Glasgow College, 1699 " This is probably a son of the Alexander Cleland who married Margaret Hamilton of Wishaw, about 1680, the Alexander who wrongfully assumed the title of "that ilk."

LIEUT.-COLONEL WILLIAM CLELAND,

Poet and Founder of the Cameronian Regiment.

This seems a fitting place to introduce the name and family of the distinguished Covenanter, William Cleland (51). His exact position in the family tree has never been unravelled; Walter Scott states that he was the father of Major William Cleland of that ilk, but, as Macaulay points out, a glance at their respective birth-dates at once disposes of this. Scott had, presumably, some definite grounds for his opinion, and it is possible that the Major was a nephew. The Covenanter is usually styled a cadet of the house.

His father was Thomas Cleland (50), garner-keeper (factor) to the Marquis of Douglas. Thomas had two sons, James (52) and William, and a daughter, whose Christian name is not known, married to Baillie Haddow, or Haddoway in Douglas, where they all resided

In the Covenanting troubles of 1678 and 1679, James and William took an active share. The latter was one of the leaders of the Covenanters at Drumclog, and much of the success of this victory over Claverhouse is attributed to him. They were both also present at Bothwell Brig, where apparently James was killed. William then passed over to Holland, where he studied law. In 1685 he took part in Argyle's Rebellion, and returned again to the Continent on its disastrous conclusion When William of Orange came over four years later, William Cleland was one of his warmest supporters It was through his energy and instrumentality that the famous Cameronian regiment, with the young Earl of Angus as Colonel, was raised in one day without beat of drum on the Holm at Douglas. Shortly afterwards the regiment, under his command, were posted at Dunkeld, and here, on the 29th August, 1689, in the moment of victory over the Highland Army, William Cleland fell in the 28th year of his age But not only as a soldier was he famous. Shortly after his

death appeared a collection of his poems, of which two are
especially noteworthy, and are quoted by Scott in his Minstrelsy, "Hollow, my fancie," and a "Description of the
Highland Host," of 1678. It is hoped soon to re-issue his
poems, accompanied by a fuller biographical account.

17th GENERATION.

MAJOR WILLIAM CLELAND (53) —Commissioner of Customs, 17th Cleland of that ilk.

"Major William Cleland, one of the Hon. Commissioners of H.M.
Customs in Scotland, lineal representative of the family of Cleland of
that ilk, Sheriff of Lanarkshire, records arms in the Lyon's Register,
Jan. 2nd, 1717." The arms are the usual ones of the family *with the
supporters*

Nisbet's Heraldry says that "Major Wm. Cleland, one
of the Commissioners of the Customs in Scotland, great-
grandson of the last-mentioned Alexander Cleland of that
ilk (14th Cleland of that ilk), carries the principal arms of
the family as a tessera of his blood and primogeniture"
(1722.) Scott states that this man was the *son* of Lt.-Col.
William Cleland, the Cameronian, but, inasmuch as the latter
was killed in 1689, at the age of 28 years, and Major Cleland
was only born in 1674 (dying at the age of 67 in 1741), when
the Cameronian would be about 13 years old, this relationship is obviously impossible. The Cameronian had, however,
an elder brother James (the two names being frequently mentioned together, and James's always first), and the Major may
have been the son of this James, Scott confounding a nephew
with a son. Since his statement is not only definite, but
appears in two different works, it is unlikely to be entirely
groundless. In Carruthers' "Life of Pope ' appears the following account of Major William Cleland :—

"To the enlarged edition of the Dunciad was prefixed a Letter to
the Publisher, dated from St. James's, and signed William Cleland
The letter is an elaborate vindication of the satire, and a censure of the
dunces, combined with unqualified praise of the moral character, the
literary aims, and genius of Pope. But no one, as Warburton asserts,
and as is abundantly proved by the contemporary prints, believed that
Cleland was the author of the letter Pope's character for artifice was
now so firmly established that all defences and appearances of this
kind were believed to emanate from himself Dennis professed not
to know whether such a 'worthy person' as William Cleland was in
existence; by another pamphleteer he was set down as a 'counterfeit
friend'; by a third he was designated as 'Pope Alexander's man
William', and by a fourth, who seems to have heard something of

C

Cleland, he is styled ' Major Sputter, a Scotch spy, who had travelled in Spain and Italy, and gathered intelligence, true or false, for ministers and others at home ' In reality, the poet's friend and shield-bearer was a gentleman who had served in the army, having, as Pope afterwards said, held the rank of major, and been under Lord Rivers in Spain He retired from the army after the peace, and (apparently on the accession of George I) obtained employment in the civil service, first as a Commissioner of Customs in Scotland, and subsequent to 1723, as a Commissioner for the Land Tax and House Duty in England. He had an official income of £500 a year, lived in St. James's Place, and associated with the Scotch Tory peers, Stair, Marchmont, etc , and was known to most of Pope's friends. In 1733 he was one of the persons in London to whom the proceedings of the Scotch peers, who met in Edinburgh in that year, were directed to be communicated. He was thus a man of some rank, and, according to Pope, he was also a man of ' universal learning and enlarged conversation.' How he submitted to such humiliations as that of lending his name to Pope whenever he wanted it is not easily accounted for. He was, we suspect, a careless, irresolute man, fond of display, and probably under personal obligations to Pope. He may also have had some share in the letters which bear his name. We may suppose that the explanatory statements, the tone of sentiment, and line of defence, were written out by Pope. His complaisant friend, knowing how tremblingly alive the poet was to all that concerned his reputation, and overpowered by his importunities, would then take up the subject, add at least part of the panegyric, and cast the whole in a somewhat freer and less author-like style. Such seems to be a reasonable conjecture as to the actual state of the case between poet and commentator They had the same feeling and tastes as to literature, politics and private society. So late as 1739, when Cleland was in his sixty-sixth year, we find Pope acknowledging the receipt of a letter from him of six pages, and, at Cleland's intercession, Pope set to the study of Don Quixote—most likely in Jervas's translation

"It is clear, however, that though Cleland had, by his subserviency, earned the poet's gratitude, he had failed to win his respect. In mentioning the letter of six pages, to which we have alluded, Pope writes to Lord Polwarth that he acknowledged the receipt of Cleland's letter, *that he might be honest even to farthings* The name of Cleland nowhere appears in the Pope and Swift correspondence, or in the conversations recorded by Spence His wife seems to have been acquainted with Swift, Lady Worsley, Miss Kelly, etc., and it is probable that the Major owed his social position, in some measure, to Mrs. Cleland's influence and connexions.*   .   .   .   .

---

* She was, we believe, related to the Proby family, mentioned in Swift's letters, and now represented by Lord Carysfort Pope presented a portrait of himself by Jervas, a three-quarters length, and a copy of the quarto Homer, to Mr Cleland, the latter inscribed in the poet's neat complimentary style · " Mr Cleland who reads all books, will please read this from his affectionate friend, A Pope " The book and picture are still at E'ten Ha'l, Hartingtonshire

Major Cleland was the representative of an old Scotch family, Cleland ' of that ilk,' distinguished for its services and alliances from the time of Wallace and Bruce William Cleland's great-grandfather (sic) sold the lands of Cleland , the house declined, and William, though well connected and educated, and, probably, proud that he was entitlèd to ' carry the principal arms of his family as a tessera of his blood and primogeniture ' *(Nisbet's Heraldry, 1722)*, was, like many of his countrymen of gentle birth but small fortune, sent into the army.

"During his early London life, Cleland is said to have been the prototype of Will Honeycomb The tradition rests on no good authority; and if it had any foundation, Steele must have altered some traits of character, and added at least twenty years to the age of the old beau for the purpose of making the ridicule stronger. Cleland was only in his thirty-eighth year when the Spectator Club was drawn He was married: and instead of despising scholars, bookish men, and philosophers, he was precisely one of this class himself The prototype of Will (though it is extremely doubtful whether the character was drawn from any particular person) is always said to have been a *Colonel* Cleland Military titles were then very carelessly applied , and if Trooper Steele could be universally known as ' Captain,' no one would have been surprised to find a gentleman who had been in the army sometimes called major, and sometimes colonel. There was, however, a Colonel Cleland contemporary with the Major, whom Swift met in Society in 1713, and who was anxious to be appointed Governor of Barbadoes. He wrote some tracts on the State of the Sugar Plantations This Colonel Cleland gave dinners to Swift, Lord Dupplin, and the other Tories, and, after the Queen's death, he entertained Lady Marlborough and Steele. But the difference between Swift's Cleland and Will Honeycomb is essential Swift described his colonel as the keenest of all place-hunters, as laying ' long traps ' to engage interest, and as ' a true Scotchman '; and we know that by a true Scotchman Swift meant everything that is most cold, crafty, and pertinacious—everything, in short, that is unlike Will Honeycomb. We must, therefore, abandon Swift's Colonel Cleland; and we do so with some regret, as we had hoped to identify him as the father of another Cleland usually connected with Pope's friend, namely, John Cleland, the unfortunate and worthless man of letters, author of an infamous novel, and an extensive miscellaneous writer

· · · · · · ·

In the Steele correspondence published by Nichols there is a letter, dated Sep 8, 1714, in which Steele mentions his intention of dining with Cleland This, we suspect, was Swift's Cleland , but on the name Cleland is the following note : " The friend and correspondent of Pope, and supposed to be the Will Honeycomb of the Spectator. Of his son, who is still living, see Anecdotes of Bowyer "

"The last days of Major Cleland seem to have been unhappy. He had for twenty years, Pope says, shown himself to be diligent, punctual and incorruptible in his office of Commissioner of Taxes, and he had no other assistance of fortune; yet he was suddenly displaced by the Minister, and died two months afterwards This harshness or injustice on the part of Walpole must, we suppose, be ascribed to politics In May, 1741, a general Parliamentary election took place; the representation of Westminster was contested with extraordinary keenness; and, though the Court candidates were returned by a small majority, the election was afterwards, on petition, declared void, and the high bailiff was censured for calling in the military and arbitrarily closing the poll-books Cleland, we suspect, would, as an elector, be found on the side of the country party He was, no doubt, known to be opposed to the administration, and such an act of contumacy in a government official, at a time when Walpole was making his last great struggle to retain office, constituted an unforgivable offence. A few more months redressed the wrong of the Westminster electors, and annihilated the power of the Minister, but, ere this time arrived, William Cleland was no more."*

In the edition of Pope's works, published in 1767, the famous " Letter to the Publisher Occasioned by the first correct Edition of the Dunciad " is signed " William Cleland, St. James's, Dec. 22, 1728 " In a note is added " This Gentleman was of Scotland, and bred at the University of Utrecht, with the Earl of Mar. He served in Spain under Earl Rivers. After the peace he was made one of the Commissioners of the Customs in Scotland, and then (after 1723) of Taxes in England; in which, having shewn himself for twenty years diligent, punctual and incorruptible, though without any other assistance of fortune, he was suddenly displaced by the Minister, in the sixty-eighth year of his age; and died two months after, in 1741. He was a person of universal learning and an enlarged conversation, no man had a warmer heart for his friend, or a sincerer attachment to the constitution of his country. And yet, for all this, the public will not allow him to be the author of this letter "

The eighth and last volume of the " Spectator " is dedicated to " Will Honeycomb."   Now, the previous volumes of the paper are dedicated to real and not to imaginary individuals, and it is surely unlikely that this should be the only instance of departure from that rule. If, moreover, Colonel William Cleland was the original of Will Honeycomb (and note that the Christian names are the same) Steele would, by dedicating this volume indirectly to him, pay a graceful compliment to one, to whom he was indebted for the

---

* On Monday last died, after a short illness, at his house in St James's Place, Major Cleland, who for many years was one of the Commissioners of the Land Tax, etc (" Daily Post " of Tuesday, September 22, 1741). Administration to his effects was granted to Lucy Cleland, his widow, October 29th.

portrayal of a most delightful personage. Were Will Honeycomb an entirely fictitious character, Steele, by a dedication
of such a nature, would miss an opportunity—one he would
be unlikely to pass by—of ingratiating some distinguished
acquaintance, or of acknowledging a friendship so useful to
him.

We may consider, then, that Will Honeycomb was not
entirely a fictitious character. Was he this Colonel Cleland?
When the " Spectator " was written in 1710 to 1714, Colonel
Cleland would only be 36 to 40 years of age, whereas in one
of the numbers Will Honeycomb is laughed at for having been
48 for the last 12 years. Now, it is probable that, if Colonel
Cleland had lived a life such as Will Honeycomb lived, he
would look and be older at 40 than his age would warrant.
Moreover, Steele would not be at all likely to adhere to strict
ages when such a fine opportunity for wit occurred as saying
that Will Honeycomb had been 48 now for the last 12 years.
This statement of the age, then, by no means militates against
the supposition that Colonel Cleland was the prototype of Will
Honeycomb, since at that time he would certainly be entering
on middle-age. Is there any other support to his claim?
Strange to say, there is in an unlooked-for situation In No.
530, Nov. 7, 1712, when Will Honeycomb writes to the Club
giving notice of his marriage to his tenant's daughter—
though she has no portion—occurs the statement that, " if
my dog of a steward had not run away, I had still been
immersed in sin and *sea-coal*. But since my late forced visit
to my estate, I am so pleased with it that I am resolved to
live and die upon it." With regard to this reference to coal,
it is rather strange to find that Hamilton of Wishaw, in
1710, mentions that "Cleland House is a good house with
convenient gardens, woods, inclosers, and *coall* "! And at
the present day there is a large coal-pit in the estate just
behind the house. However, Cleland House cannot have belonged to Major Cleland the Commissioner in 1710, since he
was, as we see, the descendant of the main branch who had
sold the estates to a cousin of the same name two generations
back ; the "Laird of Cleland, chief of that name," whom
Hamilton mentions as living in Cleland House in 1710, must
have been a descendant of the cousin who bought the place,
and was not really the chief. Probably, however, the Commissioner, though the estates of Cleland had passed out of his
hand, still retained property in the neighbourhood, much of
which is coal-bearing.

Macaulay, in his "History of England" (Vol III , Ch.

XIII) in a note points out the impossibility of the Cameronian being the father of the Commissioner, and adds, of the
latter, that he " was well known twenty years later (*i.e*, about
1709) in the literary society of London He rendered some not
very reputable services to Pope, and his son John was the
author of an infamous book but too widely circulated."

" A second Colonel Cleland (*i e*, the Commissioner), who flourished
in the *beau monde* at London, in the reign of Queen Anne and
George I, and who, besides enjoying the honour of having his
character embalmed in the ' Spectator,' under the delightful fiction
of Will Honeycomb, was the author of a letter to Pope, prefixed to
the Dunciad " *(Robert Chambers' " Lives of Eminent Scotsmen ")*

The following is the reference in Walter Scott's edition
of Swift's " Journal to Stella," 1814, to a Colonel Cleland
whom Carruthers, in the extract above quoted, considered
with much reason to be a different individual from the Commissioner of Customs. Scott's genealogical mistake in his
note has already been referred to.

London, March, 1712 —At night I dined in the city, at Pontack's,
with Lord Dupplin and some others We were treated by one Colonel
Cleland* who has a mind to be Governor of Barbadoes, and is laying
these long traps for me and others, to engage our interest for him. He
is a true Scotchman

Scott's Swift, XVIII., p. 195 —Miss Kelly's letter to Swift, Bristol,
July 8th, 1733 " I must beg the favour of you to enclose your letters
for me to William Cleland, Esq, Commissioner of Taxes, in St.
Stephen's Court, Westminster. F. A. KELLY."

Scott's Swift, XIX., p 91 —From Mrs Barber, Bath, No 3,
1736 "Lady Worsley, who heard of it (*i e*, Swift's ' Treatise in
Polite Conversation ') from Mrs. Cleland," etc. Note—Mrs. Cleland,
wife of the Colonel

Gentleman's Magazine, Vol 5, p. 620 —"Oct., 1735, William
Cleland, Esq, appointed Commissioner for the Duty on Houses "

In the Register of Wills, Somerset House, London —" Oct , 1741,
William Cleland On the twenty-ninth day, administr of the Goods
Chattels and Credits of William Cleland late of the Parish of St.
James, Westminster, in the County of Middx , Esq , deceased, was
granted to Lucy Cleland, widow of the Relict of the sd deceased,
being first sworn duly to adstr "

" Pope also made use of Cleland to write a letter to say (16 Dec.,

---

* To whom Pope inscribed the letter preliminary of the Dunciad He was the son
of Colonel Cleland, a Presbyterian poet, who wrote several hudibrastic satires in the
style of Cleveland, against the persecutors of his sect during the reigns of Charles II
and James II After the revolution, he became Colonel of what was called the
Cameronian Regiment, at the head of which he was killed at Dunkeld in 1689. His
son, here mentioned, was the intimate of Pope, Swift, and the wits of Queen Anne's
time , and had himself a son, too well known as the author of the most infamous
book in the English language. In this singular pedigree, a fanatic poet begets a free
living wit, and he, a gentleman of character and fashion, has a son who merited the
pillary.

1731) in contradiction of the report that 'Timon' was intended for James Brydges, Duke of Chandos. . . . Pope (3 Nov., 1730) asks Lord Oxford to recommend a son of Cleland, who was then at Christ Church, having been elected from Westminster in 1728." *(Stephen's "Dict of Nat. Biogr")*

The reference amongst Steele's Letters (edited by Nichols, 1787, Vol. I., p 114, No. ccvii) to Colonel Cleland, mentioned above by Carruthers, consists of this :—

(To Mrs. Steele)

" Dear Prue,   Sep 8, 1714.
    I shall dine at Clelands, in order to see Lady Marlborough as soon as she is at leisure after dinner   I have spoken to two or three of the justices, and I think all will do well. Your most obedient husband, RICHARD STEELE "

The following is extracted from " Notes and Queries," 1866 :—

    " The ' Gentleman's Magazine ' notices his death thus ·—' Major Wm Cleland, Sept , 1741, aet 67, a Commissioner of the House-tax, a place of £500 a-year !   .   .   . Curiously enough there were three William Clelands, all Commissioners : Major Wm Cleland, mentioned above as head of the family, Captain Wm. Cleland, R N., of Knownoblehill and Tapely; and this last, Major Wm. Cleland, the friend of Pope Swift mentions him and his wife, several times, with great respect, in his Diary to Stella; and with anything but respect a Colonel Cleland, whom he describes as 'a true Scotchman,' and as intriguing for the governorship of Barbadoes (Swift, Journal, March 30, 1712-13, ed. Sir Walter Scott). The note to this passage goes on to confound this Colonel with the Major Cleland; but he really was son of James Cleland of Stonepath, Peebles (see his will, Aug 24, 1718, proved in London) , and as it appears, got the Barbadoes appointment and died in a very few years. The heraldries give the arms of Clelland of Barbadoes differenced from those of the head of the family "

    " HIS SISTER, who died in 1733, married Thos Hamilton of Newton, now represented by the Rev. J. Hamilton-Gray of Carntyne." Quoted from " Burke's Commoners," old edition, by a writer in " Notes and Queries," 1866 " Thomas Hamilton, of Newton, who m. the sister of Major Clelland, representative of the ancient family of Clelland of Clelland in Lanarkshire, and by her, who died in 1733, had issue.   I. James, his heir, II John.   I. Dorothea, m. to Andrew Gray of Wellhouse II. Elizabeth, m to William Gray, brother of Andrew Gray " *(Burke's Commoners, Vol. III., p. 11. Ed. 1838)*

18th GENERATION.

JOHN CLELAND (54).—Supposed to be the son of Major William Cleland, 17th Cleland of that ilk, 1709-1789. The "Gentleman's Magazine" for 1789, p. 180, thus notices his death :—

Jan. 23, 1789.—In Petty France, aged 80, John Cleland, Esq. He was the son of Col C , that celebrated fictitious member of the Spectator's Club, whom Steele describes under the name of Will Honeycombe. A portrait of him hung up in the son's library till his death, which indicates all the manners and *d'abord* of the fashionable town-rake at the beginning of this century. The son, with the scatterings of his father's fortune, and some share of his dissipations, after passing through the forms of a good education at Westminster-college, where he was admitted in 1722, at the age of 13, and was contemporary with Lord Mansfield, went as consul to Smyrna, where, perhaps, he first imbibed those loose principles which, in a subsequent publication, too infamous to be particularised, tarnished his reputation as an author. On his return from Smyrna he went to the East Indies; but quarreling with some of the members of the presidency of Bombay, he made a precipitate retreat from the East, with little or no benefit to his fortunes Being without profession or any settled means of subsistence, he soon fell into difficulties, a prison, and its miseries, were the consequences. In this situation, one of those booksellers who disgrace the profession, offered him a temporary relief for writing the work* above alluded to, which brought a stigma on his name, which time has not obliterated, and which will be consigned to his memory whilst its poisonous contents are in circulation. For this publication he was called before the privy council; and the circumstance of his distress being known, as well as his being a man of some parts, John Earl Granville, the then president, nobly rescued him from the like temptation, by getting him a pension of £100 per year, which he enjoyed to his death, and which had so much the desired effect, that, except "The Memoirs of a Coxcomb," which has some smack of dissipated manners, and "The Man of Honour," written as an amende honourable for his former exceptionable book, Mr. C mostly dedicated his time to political and philological publications, and was the author of the *long* letters given in the public prints, from time to time, signed a Briton, Modestus, &c , &c , and of some curious tracts on the Celtic language He lived within the income from his pension for many years, in a retired situation in Petty France, surrounded by a good library, and the occasional visits of some literary friends, to whom he was a very agreeable companion, and died at the advanced age of 82 (sic). In conversation he was very pleasant and anecdotical, understanding most of the living languages, and speaking them all

---

* The sum given for the copy of this work was twenty guineas. The sum received fo the sale could not he less than £10,000.

very fluently. As a writer, he shewed himself best in novels, song-writing, and the lighter species of authorship; but when he touched politics, he touched it like a torpedo, he was cold, benumbing, and soporific

"John Cleland is represented as having been the son of "Colonel Cleland," and we should be glad to be able to divorce him from all connexion with the retired Major and literary Commissioner of the land-tax The evidence on the other side is, however, notwithstanding the erroneous military designation, strong and almost conclusive While John Cleland was living it was twice asserted in print that he was the son of Pope's friend and correspondent Nichols, who asserted this, was a diligent collector of facts and eminently versed in the literary gossip of the eighteenth century. He had the best means of obtaining information as to this particular point, and his evidence never having been, so far as we know, contradicted, must be received as decisive. He is supported also by Isaac Reed, editor of the " European Magazine " (vol. xv), who mentions John Cleland as the son of Colonel Cleland; " whose name is to a letter prefixed to the Dunciad." Nichols and Reed, apparently, did not know that there were two military Clelands, contemporaries in London, but they both knew that John's father was Pope's friend.

In the Anecdotes of Bowyer (1782), John Cleland's father is stated to have been a colonel, and the friend and correspondent of Pope. John Cleland died in Westminster, January 23rd, 1789, aged eighty. A memoir of him appeared in the "Gentleman's " and " Scots " Magazines for February, and there he is again represented as the son of Colonel Cleland, and the original of Will Honeycomb, and it is mentioned that a portrait of the father, in the fashionable costume of the beginning of the century, always hung in the son's library It is not stated in this memoir that Colonel Cleland was the friend and correspondent of Pope, but when Nichols adopted the memoir in a note to his second edition of his Anecdotes of Bowyer, he inserted this fact

At his father's death . . . . when administration to his effects was granted his widow, Lucy Cleland, in 1741, the son, we suppose, was then abroad, having gone to Smyrna, it is said, in some mercantile adventure, and afterwards to the East Indies. We find that he was a Westminster scholar, having been elected in 1722, but he left the same year. One Henry Cleland—probably another son of the Major's—was elected in 1725. ' *(Carruthers' " Life of Pope ")*

In Welch's " *Alumni Westmonasteriensis*," 1852, appears the following .—

A D 1722, 24th April, Election Tuesday. Admitted into St. Peter's College,   .   .   age 11, John Cleland, abiit (1723).

NOTE.—J. Cleland, the son of Col Cleland, from whom Steele drew the celebrated character of Will Honeycomb in the " Spectator."

Here follows a short summary of his doings " It is said that he was an agreeable companion, and his conversation full of anecdotes, and he also understood and spoke fluently most modern languages. He died at the advanced age of 80, on the 23rd Jan , 1789. He was brother to H Cleland (election, 1728).

A D 1725, admitted into St Peter's College, age 13, Henry Cleland, Oxford, 1728

NOTE —H. Cleland, brother to John (Admissions, 1722)—Weston, Indentures. In a " List of the Captains of each election, as admitted to college," under *1704* appears " Hen. Cleland " This date must be erroneous, a previous date is acknowledged to be wrong (p. 533). The above make John Cleland, b 1711 , Henry Cleland, b 1712

" Bowyer published in 1765 ' The Way to Things by Words and to Words by Things,' by Mr John Cleland, 8vo This publication was followed, in 1768, by ' Specimens of an Etimological* Vocabulary, or Essay, by Means of the Analitic* Method. to retrieve the antient Celtic ' ; with ' A View of a Literary Plan, for the retrieval of the antient Celtic; in aid of an Explanation of various Points of Antiquity in general, and of the Antiquities of Great Britain and Ireland in particular,' and Proposals for publishing by subscription, in two volumes quarto, ' The Celtic Retrieved, by the Analitic Method, or Reduction to Radicals; illustrated by a Glossary of various, and especially British Antiquities,' and in 1769 by ' Additional Articles to the Specimen,' etc In these publications Mr Cleland has displayed a great fund of ingenuity and erudition, not unworthy the education he received at Westminster In the Proposals for continuing his Celtic labours, he says, " As to the recourse to a subscription, I have no apology to make for it, but one, which is, that it is necessary, as being the only one. Not that I am insensible of there being many and just objections to this method, but the candour of a liberal construction will hardly rank among them its being liable to an abuse This is no more than what it has in common with the best of things Whoever considers the vast comprehensiveness of this plan, and the aids of all kinds which it must, to have justice done to it, indispensably and implicitly require, will easily allow the undertaking to be not only impossible to a small private fortune but even where there might be a large one, the work itself to imply so much of proposed utility to the publick, as not to be without some right to solicit the assistance of the publick. It was the failure of that assistance, that, probably lost to it one of presumably the most useful and valuable works that any language or any nation could have had to boast of, the second part of ' The British Archæology,' of one of our greatest and solidist Antiquaries, Edward Llhuyd, who, or suppressed, or dropped, or, at least, did not effectually carry it on, from his disgust or discouragement, at his having been forced to publish the first part at his own heavy expense a loss this to the British republic of letters hardly reparable ! Need I mention the celebrated Dr. Hyde's boiling his

' The writer's C ι ι has swallowed up his *Greek* '—T F.

tea-kettle, with almost the whole impression left on his hands, of that profoundly learned treatise of his, ' De Religione Veterum Persarum,' admired by all literary Europe, and neglected at home, so low was the taste for literature in this country, already sunk ! For the re-publication of this work, we have now, however, the obligation to the public spirit of Dr. Sharpe, that patron and promoter of literature, of which himself is at once an ornament, a judge, and a support, with the greater merit of his not deserting it in its present state of disgrace. With so cold, so unpromising a prospect before me, and very justly conscious of not only an uncomparably less title to favourable opinion, but of having much more to apologise for, than of any merit to plead, I have only, in extenuation of my presumption to address the publick under such disadvantages, one solemn and unaffected truth to offer, and this it is. Finding this retrieval of the Celtic (that language actually existing nowhere as a language, and everywhere as the root of all or most of the languages in Europe, dead or living, modern or antient, and entering into the composition of almost every word that we now, at this instant, use in common conversation; finding, I say, the retrieval of this elementary, or mother-tongue, at least included in Proposals from more than one foreigner, I have thought it my duty to form a wish, that it might not be my fault, if the British publick was not, as early as other countries, in possession of the benefit of such a retrieval, for the satisfactory elucidation of some of the most interesting British antiquities But how far I may find the publick disposed to second that wish, or to enable me to fulfil it, must remain entirely at the discretion of that publick J.C." *(" Nichol's Literary Anecdotes of Bowyer," 1812, Vol. 11 , pp 456, 457)*

Nichols then proceeds to copy the account of John Cleland, which appeared in the " Gentleman's Magazine," 1789, when he died, though he gives no reference to it. " Cleland's excuse before the Privy Council was poverty. The Bookseller gave him only £20 for it, and is said to have received £20,000 I make little doubt of his correcting Lady Mary Wortley Montague's letters, copying them from Lowden, and publishing them. T. F " *(Note to p 458 of Vol 11., of Nichols' " Lit Anecdotes ")*

" In 1750 he published ' Fanny Hill,' . . . . a first part had appeared previously in 1748, and a second in 1749. In 1751 Memoirs of a Coxcomb, a work of greater merit   .   No punishment was inflicted on Cleland, but a bookseller (Drybutter), who is said to have altered the language of the book for the worse after it had been favour-ably noticed in the ' Monthly Review ' (ii., 451-2), was made to stand in the pillory in 1757.   . . ' The Way to Things by Words and to Words by Things,' to which is added a succinct account of the Sanscrit, or the learned language of the Brahmins; also two essays, the one on the Origin of the Musical Waits at Christmas, the other on the Real Secret of the Freemasons, London, 1766, 8vo .   . ' Sur-prises of Love,' London, 1765, 12mo, and ' The Man of Honour,' Lon-don, 17—, 12mo , 3 vols " *(Leslie Stephen's " Dict of Nat Biogr.")*

" In support of my statement about Mr. Griffiths, see Monthly Review II , 431, March, 1750. . . . . The book to which I allude is that which was written by the son of a Colonel Cleland, who is generally supposed to have been Pope's Cleland, but is more likely to have been his brother or cousin. Pope's friend is described always as Major Cleland A letter from his infamous descendant or kingsman is printed in the Garrick Correspondence, I , 56-59." *(John Forster's " Life of Goldsmith," 1854, Vol. I., xxx.)*

HENRY CLELAND (55).—Mentioned above in Welch's *" Alumni Westmonasteriensis."* Supposed to be a son of Major William Cleland.

JAMES CLELAND (56), in Crossford. Married Anne Smellie about 1731 or 1735. Born about 1710-1715.

His youngest son, Robert's, wife used to speak of the gallant appearance he made on horseback with his family as they rode into or out of Lanark, near which they lived, apparently at Mouse Mill.

MOUSE MILL —This is said to have been the last property owned in the neighbourhood of the ancestral estates by the Clelands of Cleland. Here probably John Cleland W S , died in 1777. The House of Mouse Mill still stands about two miles from Lanark on the Mouse near Cartland Crags, and just beside the old Roman Bridge. Its situation is very picturesque, and just on the opposite side of the river Mouse is the mill from which it receives its name.

This James Cleland's relationship to Major William Cleland, Commissioner of Customs, is not exactly known. By some he is said to have been a son, others consider him a nephew A very unreliable source states that he was the son of James Cleland, elder brother of the Cameronian, William Cleland; he is much more likely to have been a grandson, however; we have already mentioned that Major William Cleland himself may have been a son of James Cleland, the Covenanter. Whatever the relationship is, and this James Cleland's grand-daughter, Miss Annie Haldane writes, that " one of the Clelands, she did not know whether her great-grandfather or not, was Commissioner in the Customs," it was something very close, for in 1800, sixty years after the Commissioner's death, we find that Walter Cleland, grandson of James Cleland, claims to be the head of the family. He directed a John Brown, of 23, Carnaby St., Carnaby Sq , London, to investigate his claim to the honours of the family, who writes to him thus on March 4th .—" Sir,—In compliance to your request I have perused Nisbet's Heraldry and other books respecting the ancient family of Cleland; and have been enabled to send you the annexed account, which has been faithfully transcribed. This being an age when justice and equity are done to the claimants of titles and estates, I see nothing, sir, to prevent you from applying for the honours of that family in your person; of which you are so conspicuous a branch. Hoping, sir, my researches will meet with your approbation, I am with the greatest esteem, Sir, Your most obliged and most humble servant, John Brown."

This is sealed with the seal of the Clelands of Cleland containing supporters indicating a head of the family In the abstract, Major William Cleland, Commissioner of Customs, is mentioned as being the Cleland of Cleland of his day. Walter Cleland must have been his great-grandson: it never seems to have entered Walter's mind to make out any genealogical tree, probably because the names and dates of death of his father, grandfather, and great-grandfather were so comparatively recent as to render this unnecessary Surely, had his grandfather, James Cleland, been other than the eldest son leaving issue of the Major Cleland, Commissioner of Customs, Walter Cleland would have left record of the fact, and of the means by which he claimed the honours of the family.

For more than a hundred years now there has been a rumour that a latent baronetcy existed in the family, to which Walter Cleland and his descendants were entitled Walter's letter above quoted seems to be connected with an investigation into this. It has been said that Walter or his son William Lennox Cleland had proved their right to such a title to their own satisfaction, and were on the point of having the matter legally investigated when a bank crisis rendered such efforts impossible. John Fullarton Cleland, in his lifetime, was said to be entitled to the baronetcy, but neither through him, nor by any other means have I ever been able to ascertain on what grounds the claim was based. It cannot be connected with "Sir James Cleland of Monkland, Knt," of James VI.'s reign, since he is never styled a "banneret" and was not a Cleland of that ilk. Strange to say, a Col. J H. Cleland, writing in 1831, and styling himself a descendant of Major William Cleland through the Clelands of Carnbee, refers to this dormant baronetcy also.

19th GENERATION.

JOHN CLELAND (57), W S., 19th Cleland of Cleland — 1735-1777. Died at Lanark, 8th April, 1777, aged 41 years.

" John, son to James Cleland and Anne Smellie in Crossford, bapt. March 6, 1735." *(Reg. Lesmahago.)* According to one statement, " John Cleland and Mary Muter were married at Edinboro' by the Rev. John Glen, 14th February, 1758. They had six children : Mary Muter died at Edin. 26th April, 1767, aged 27 years." In the City Parish Register at Edinburgh appears this notice of the marriage : " John Clelland, writer, and Miss Mary Mutter, daughter of the deceased Robert Mutter, merchant in South Leith, now both in the Tron Kirk. March 5th, 1758."

John Cleland, late writer in Lanark, has his testament confirmed, 29th November, 1790. *(Commiss. of Lanark.)*

" My father's father, John Cleland, was unfortunately most extravagant He was a Writer to the Signet in Edinburgh. He had originally a good fortune, but for his amusement used to be in the habit of buying dilapidated country places, putting them in beautiful order, and when his improvements were finished, sold them immediately and bought others. He was also wrapped up in music. I knew in Edinburgh an old gentleman of the name of Stoddart who was well acquainted with him, also a great musical genius. He told me he was remarkably handsome and elegant and a very fine player on the violin. He also kept many fine hunters, even when he was so poor that he had scarcely anything to give them to eat. He died at Lanark, 8th April. 1777, 41 years of age." *(Extract from letter of Mrs. Herring—Catherine Cleland)*

MARGARET CLELAND (61).—Sister. Born 1736. Married Dr Haldane of Edinburgh, and had four sons and a daughter, viz , John, William, George, James, Annie. Mrs. Haldane afterwards married Dr Morris at Bristol, then Mr. Zeigler in London She left no issue by her two last marriages. Mrs Herring in a note refers to old Miss Annie Haldane as giving her the information that one of the Clelands was Commission of Customs. (1866.)

JAMES CLELAND (59).—Brother. Was a ship chandler in London. Was married and had issue, but none survived. Born 1737.

WILLIAM CLELAND (58).—Born 1742. Brother of John Cleland W.S. Married Miss Johnstone, daughter of a Col. Johnstone, and had issue, but none survived

MARY CLELAND (60).—Born 1745.

ROBERT CLELAND (62).—Youngest brother of John Cleland, W S. Born 1748. Died about 1800. Married Janet Agnes Wingate. daughter of Rev. J. Wingate by his wife Janet, daughter and heiress of James Fenton of Millearn, Perthshire. Left issue, four sons, James, Robert, John and William.

ANNE CLELAND (63).—Born 1749, married Rev J Porteous.

CLELANDS OF CARNBEE, FIFESHIRE.

1st GENERATION.

COLONEL ROBERT "CLEILAND" (64), of Carnbee, is said to have been a grandson of Major Cleland, head of the family. *(Writer in " Notes and Queries.")* He died in 1760, in command of H.M. 63rd Foot, then stationed at Guadaloupe. He left two sons.

2nd GENERATION.

(a) ROBERT CLEILAND (65), elder son. Lieutenant R N. (3rd Lieut. H.M. "Fame," in Rodney's action, April 12th, 1782). Was twice married. By his first wife he had three sons, who all died young. By his second wife, with two daughters, he had an only son, William Douglas Cleiland.

(b) MOLESWORTH CLEILAND (66) —Lieutenant R.A. Was killed in America in 1777

3rd GENERATION.

LIEUT-GENERAL WILLIAM DOUGLAS CLELAND (67) —Son of Robert Cleland　Appointed to the Bengal Army, December 28th, 1798. He died February 26th, 1848; his wife, Mary, April 2nd, 1839　He held the office of principal registrar of the diocese of Sarum, in the gift of Bishop Douglas.

4th GENERATION.

COL. J. H. CLELAND (68).—Probably a son of William Douglas Cleland, since he claims Col. Robert Cleland as his grandfather. Resided at 58, Welbeck Street, Cavendish Square, London, in 1831.

On August 5th, 1752, HANS CLELAND (69), late of Carnbee, married Jacobina, only child of James Moir, of Earnshaw, Esq　In 1747 he had been appointed ensign to a Scottish regiment raised for the service of the States-General of Holland

(Clelands of Carnbee.—Writer in "Notes and Queries" refers to Burke's "Heraldic Illustrations," Dodwell and Miles' "Indian Army," "Scot's Magazine," "Gentleman's Magazine.")

CLELANDS OF THE 20th GENERATION.

DESCENDANTS OF JOHN CLELAND, W.S., 19th CLELAND OF
CLELAND.

ROBERT CLELAND (70).—Born 14th November, 1758.
Apparently unmarried. Left no issue.

JAMES CLELAND (71).—Born 5th February, 1760. No
issue.

JOHN CLELAND (72).—Born 10th April, 1761   Died 1800
Unmarried. A sailor. Died in India from lockjaw, brought
on by cutting his thumb. He was in his fortieth year. He
left part of his money to his uncle, Robert Cleland's family.
He and his brother Walter, their father dying when they were
children, were brought up in their uncle Robert Cleland's
family.

WALTER CLELAND (73).—Born 29th March, 1763, " Being
the day on which peace was proclaimed at Edinburgh between
Great Britain and France." Married a daughter of Sir Paul
Jodrell, 1st Bart.; and had issue, William (21st Cleland of
Cleland), Catherine, and a boy who died in infancy. He was
a banker, and amassed a moderate fortune.

MARY CLELAND (74).—Born 19th January, 1764.   No
issue.

WILLIAM CLELAND (75).—Born 6th September, 1766.   No
issue

21st GENERATION.

WILLIAM LENNOX CLELAND (76) —21st Cleland of that ilk.
Married Henrietta Fullarton (Foulerton). Graduated M A.,
Edin., 1st April, 1819. *(Cat. of Edin. Graduates.)* He was
left an orphan while quite a young man, and became an inmate
of the Earl of Buchan's house, with whom was a family friendship. At the age of 18 he was able to support himself by contributions to the great Reviews (the Quarterly and Edinburgh) of the day, a feat which indicates considerable literary
ability on his part. He went out to India and became a barrister and comfortably off He was drowned crossing the
Hoogley. At or about the time of death his wife was sitting in
a garden when a white owl flew past her, and an uncomfortable
feeling of dread seized her, from which she augured that
something unfortunate had happened to her husband, which
was confirmed later by news from India For this reason the
appearance of a white owl was supposed to be of evil omen to
members of the family; whether this was its first appearance,

however, in that guise, or whether previous generations had experienced its baneful presence, I cannot say

His wife, HENRIETTA FULLARTON, married later a Dr Glen, whose daughter by a previous marriage became the wife of John Cleland, Henrietta's son. Henrietta lived to an old age, dying in 1875, at Beaumont, near Adelaide. She was descended from the old family of the Fullartons of Fullarton, through George Fullarton, of Broughton Hall, and was first cousin to the 12th Earl of Buchan and second cousin to Lord Elphinstone.

CATHERINE CLELAND (77) (Mrs Herring).—Sister of Wm. Cleland. One daughter—Anne Zoe Herring

INFANT.—Died.

22nd GENERATION.

JOHN FULLERTON CLELAND (78).—22nd Cleland of Cleland. John Fullerton Cleland, only son of William Cleland and Henrietta Fullerton, and great-grandson of John Cleland W.S. (1736-1777), was born in 1821, and died at the age of eighty years in Adelaide in 1901. He and his elder sister Margaret were left orphans and comfortably off when quite young. Their trustee, however, made them wards in Chancery, and by this means most of their capital was swallowed up. While a youth he went as a midshipman on a voyage of one of the East India Company's ships, but not caring for such a life left their service. He was afterwards for a short while at Oxford and at the Nonconformist School at Cheshunt. After his marriage in 1845, at Norham, England, with Miss Elizabeth Glen, daughter of Dr. Glen, a London physician, he went out to Hong Kong and Canton in 1846, as a missionary. William Lennox Cleland, his eldest son, was born during their residence here. While working at Canton, John Cleland received a severe sun-stroke, the evil effects of which he never really overcame. This necessitated his return to England, where he lived for some while at Taunton, and while in this country George Fullerton and an elder son and daughter, Walter and Mary, who both died young, were born. John Cleland's sister and her husband, Samuel Davenport, having at this time taken up a grant of land in South Australia, John Cleland and his wife and children were induced to join them. This they did in 1852, and dwelt first in Fernhill Cottage, then in a larger wooden house, Gleville, at Beaumont, near Adelaide. He obtained the Government post of Registrar of Births, Marriages, and Deaths, and held this office for many years. His

D

four younger sons were born in this house, which stands (or rather stood, being pulled down in 1903), surrounded by vineyards on the hillside at Beaumont overlooking the plains of Adelaide. His wife died in 1895, he himself in 1901, six years later.

He was a man always studiously inclined and a great reader; he collected around him a good library, but never gave to the world as a writer any of the literary material he had assimilated. He was buried beside his wife in the Walkerville Cemetery, near Adelaide

ELIZABETH GLEN.—Married John Fullerton Cleland She was a daughter of — GLEN, M.D., a physician of London. Her brothers were Alec Glen and Tom Glen, who died unmarried in Australia, and George Glen, who married Millicent Short, daughter of Augustus Short, 1st Bishop of Adelaide (three sons, five daughters). Her sister, Caroline Glen, became, first, Mrs. Barnett (son and two daughters, all unmarried), and later Mrs. Greenway (no issue).

MARGARET CLELAND (79).—Married Mr., afterwards Sir Samuel Davenport, K C.M.G. Samuel Davenport, in the forties, took up some land near Adelaide, S. Australia. He and his wife journeyed thither by sailing vessel, *viâ* Tasmania. At Hobart they had to charter a whaling schooner to convey them to Adelaide, the captain of the vessel stipulating that he was to be allowed to catch any whales seen. Sure enough, they captured one, and reached Adelaide with the decks covered with blubber. Samuel Davenport was one of South Australia's most distinguished colonists and a personal friend of most of her Governors, especially Sir George Grey; Captain Sturt, the explorer, was also a great friend. At one time he was Minister for Crown Lands. He represented South Australia as Commissioner at several international exhibitions, and was knighted in 1887 Lady Davenport and her husband were always the greatest companions and delightful conversationists She died in 1900.

ANNE ZOE HERRING.

23rd GENERATION.

WILLIAM LENNOX CLELAND, 23rd Cleland of Cleland.

WILLIAM LENNOX CLELAND (80).—Eldest son of John Fullerton Cleland and his wife, Elizabeth Glen. Was born in Hong Kong on January 18th, 1847. Shortly after his birth, his parents returned to England, and after a year or so's residence there departed for Australia. William Lennox Cleland as a boy was greatly in the company of his aunt, Mrs. (later Lady) Davenport, who had no children of her own, and who gave him most of his early education. As a lad he saw a little of bush life, driving cattle overland from Port Augusta (South Australia) to Adelaide, with an uncle, Alec Glen. Later he spent a year on Dr. Kelly's vineyard at MacLaren Vale, learning the manufacture of wine and studying the vine Previous to this he had spent a few months at school, in 1862, at Berne, Switzerland, when Mr. and Mrs Davenport were visiting Europe. In 1872 he left Adelaide for Edinburgh to study medicine, taking there his degrees of M B , Ch.M., in 1876. He was appointed House Surgeon to Professor Annandale in 1876. While there he married Mattie Burton, daughter of John Hill Burton, LL.D., Historiographer Royal for Scotland, on June 21st, 1877. They returned to Australia immediately, and William Lennox spent a year or so in private practice. On June 22nd, 1878, their elder son, John Burton Cleland, was born; on July 19th, 1882, William Lauder Cleland. In 1878 William Lennox Cleland was appointed Medical Officer to the Parkside Lunatic Asylum, succeeding to the post of Colonial Surgeon to South Australia in 1896 He also held the position of Lecturer in Materia Medica at the Adelaide University for many years, in 1902 resigning this to assume the duties of Lecturer in Insanity and Medical Jurisprudence. He was also for many years Secretary to the Royal Society of South Australia, President of it for the years 1898-1900, and afterwards a Vice-President. In 1890 he was President of the South Australian Branch of the British Medical Association, and in 1900 was President of the Section of Mental Science and Education at the Australasian Association for the Advancement of Science.

MATTIE BURTON, wife of William Lennox Cleland, was the third daughter of Dr. John Hill Burton, Historiographer Royal for Scotland, and Isabella Lauder, his wife Dr. Hill Burton was a well-known and distinguished literary man of Edinburgh between the years 1840 and 1880, when he died. He was author of "The Book-Hunter," "History of Scotland," "Scot Abroad," "Life of Simon, Lord Lovat," etc., and edited the Register of the Privy Council of Scotland. He was a friend of Professor Spalding, Lord Cockburn, Lord Jeffrey, Cosmo Innes, and many other Edinburgh worthies, and corresponded with Macaulay and Thomas Carlyle His father had been a Lieutenant William Burton, and his mother a Miss Paton, of the Patons of Grandholm, near Aberdeen. This Miss Paton's mother was a Miss Lance, a descendant of the

Lances, Temples and Nelsons. Dr Hill Burton's first wife, Isabella Lauder, was a daughter of Captain Lauder.

WALTER CLELAND (81).—Died young.

MARY CLELAND (82)—Died young.

GEORGE FULLERTON CLELAND (83).—Second surviving son of John F. Cleland. Born in England in 1852. Married Miss Amy Giles, daughter of Henry Giles of Adelaide, merchant, in 1878. As a young man he assisted his uncle, Samuel Davenport, in growing vines and making wine, later becoming a prominent Adelaide wine-maker. Four sons and six daughters Lived at Adelaide since marriage

ELPHINSTONE DAVENPORT CLELAND (84).—Fourth son of John Fullerton Cleland, was born 5th December, 1854. He was sheep-station manager, journalist, and subsequently attorney and general manager for foreign mining companies. He was the author of " The White Kangaroo," which was first published in a magazine called " Sunday," and then published in book form. He also wrote several serial and short stories for the " Australasian," " Adelaide Observer," and " Sydney Mail." The names of the principal of them are " A Life's Punishment," " Winninowie," " Life on the Barrier," " A Spray of Honeysuckle," " A Bygone Crime." He also wrote numerous shorter stories, articles, etc., including many written for Cassell's " Picturesque Australasia."

He married, first, Susanna Blood, only daughter of Walter Davies, formerly of County Galway, Ireland, now of Adelaide, South Australia. They had three children, Elizabeth, born 1879 ; Walter, born 1881, died 1883 ; and Samuel, born 1885. His second wife is Anne, younger daughter of the Rev. Donald Mackinnon, Kilbride, Isle of Skye By her he has two children, Donald, born 1901, and William, born 1903.

CHARLES ALEXANDER CLELAND (85).—Born December, 1865 Became a surveyor under the Government. Married Ethel Mary Dutton, daughter of Mrs. Dutton, of Lucindale, S.E of South Australia, 1891 No children Before marriage he was in the field surveying in the South-East, but after marriage was in the Surveyor-General's Office in Adelaide. In 1899 accepted the post of surveyor to a gold-mine at Lawlers, West Australia, but returned to Adelaide in 1900

ALLAN FRASER CLELAND (86)—Born June, 1867. Married Mabel Gardner in 1894. An engineer ; first engaged in the construction of the Overland Railway at Hergott Springs, etc., South Australia ; later, in the construction of a railway in West Australia. In 1899 he settled at Stanthorpe, in Queensland, and started a fruit orchard. No children.

EDWARD ERSKINE CLELAND (87).—Born April, 1869. Married in 1893 Edith Auld, daughter of Patrick Auld, who accompanied John MacDougall Stuart, the explorer, across the Continent of Australia. Graduated LL.B., Adelaide University in 1890 Became a junior member of the firm of Symon, Bakewell and Rounsevell, whose most prominent member, Sir Josiah Symon, is one of the leading members of the South Australian Bar, as well as a prominent politician in the Federal Parliament.

24th GENERATION.

Children of William Lennox Cleland (23rd Cleland of Cleland) and Mattie Burton.

1 JOHN BURTON CLELAND (88).—Born June 22nd, 1878. Studied three first years of medical course at Adelaide University (1895-1897); last two at Sydney (1898-1899). Received degrees of M.B., Ch M., Sydney University, 1900 House Surgeon, Prince Alfred Hospital, Sydney, 1900. Resident Pathologist and Senior Resident Medical Officer, 1901 Voyage to Manila, China, and Japan, 1903 Demonstrator in Pathology at Sydney University, 1902 Visit to Great Britain, 1903. Cancer Research Scholar, London Hospital, 1904-1905

2. WILLIAM LAUDER CLELAND (89).—Born July 19th, 1882. Studied Science Course, Adelaide University, 1900-1905. B.Sc , 1904 In 1902, volunteered for last contingent to South African War, and went as Sergeant, but war ended before his arrival in South Africa.

Children of George Fullerton Cleland and Amy Giles.

1. HENRY FULLERTON CLELAND (90).—Born August, 1878. Educated at Prince Alfred College Entered his father's business office. Died September 13th, 1904

2. LESLIE GLEN CLELAND (91) —Born in 1880.

3 MARGARET FRASER CLELAND (92) —Born 1882.

4. GLADYS OLIVE CLELAND (93).—Born 1885.

5 DULCIBEL ERSKINE CLELAND (94) —Born 1887

6 JOAN JOCELYN CLELAND (95).—Born 1889.

7 AMY BEATRICE CLELAND (96).—Born 1890

8. GEORGE FULLERTON CLELAND (97) —Born 1892.

9 UNA PHYLLIS CLELAND (98) —Born, 1894.

10 DORIS ISABEL CLELAND (99).—Born 1896

11. HAROLD CLELAND (100) —Born 1898.

Children of Elphinstone Davenport Cleland and Susan Davis.

1. ELIZABETH CLELAND (101)—Born December, 1879. Lived with her parents at Adelaide, Broken Hill, Coolgardie (West Australia).

2. WALTER CLELAND (102)—Born 1881, died 1883.

3. SAMUEL DAVENPORT CLELAND (103).—Born 1885. Educated at St. Peter's College, Adelaide. Learning mining engineering.

And Anne MacKinnon (2nd wife).

4. DONALD MACKINNON CLELAND (104)—Born 1901.

5 WILLIAM CLELAND (105).—Born 1903.

Children of Edward Erskine Cleland and Edith Auld.

1. TOM ERSKINE CLELAND (106)—Born 1894.

2. ISABEL ERSKINE CLELAND (107) ("Bobs")—Born 1900.

3. AUDREY ERSKINE CLELAND (108)—Born September, 1903.

CLELANDS OF THE 20th GENERATION.

Children of Robert Cleland and Janet Wingate

JAMES CLELAND (109)—Born about 1777. Unmarried. As a young man entered the East India Company's service, and was amongst the missing at the Siege of Seringapatam in 1799, when General Sir David Baird, with Col. Wellesley, afterwards Duke of Wellington, in command of the Reserves, stormed the fort of Tippoo Sahib.

ROBERT CLELAND (110).—Unmarried. In a bank at Edinburgh Buried in the West Church, Edinburgh.

JOHN CLELAND (111)—Born 1795. Died at Perth, 2nd January, 1836. Appointed Assistant Surgeon to the 1st Dragoon Guards at the age of eighteen, was sent to the Peninsular War, and arrived there the day after the battle of Vittoria, but in time to attend to the wounded. Then accompanied his regiment to Ireland and Canada. Settled as surgeon in Perth, and married there, on the 23rd April, 1832, Jean Caw, daughter of John Caw, Lord Provost of Perth. Contracted typhus fever from a poor family he was attending, and under this rapidly sank and died.

WILLIAM CLELAND (112).—Born 1798. Died at Madeira in 1840 Married Mary Henderson, daughter of Robert Henderson and sister of Thomas Wingate Henderson, of Roke Manor, Hants. Manager of the Royal Bank in Perth.

CLELANDS OF THE 21st GENERATION.

Children of John Cleland and Jane Caw.

ROBERT CLELAND (113).—Born at Perth, 15th December, 1833   Married in Canada Elizabeth Freeman, daughter of John Freeman, Dublin, on 1st November, 1866   She died in 1893   He was educated at the High School, Edinburgh ; lived many years in Canada, and is now resident in London   The author of several novels (*vide* Bibliography, at the end of this volume), and a painter in water-colours.

JOHN CLELAND (114), M.D., L R C S.E , LL.D. (St Andrew's and Edinburgh), D Sc. (Q U I.), F R S , Regius Professor of Anatomy in the University of Glasgow. Born in Perth, 15th June, 1835, the second son of John Cleland, Surgeon (a descendant of the old family of Cleland of Cleland, Lanarkshire), who began life as Hospital Assistant in the Peninsular War, and was afterwards for some years Assistant Surgeon in the First Dragoons (The Royals)   Professor Cleland's mother was Jean, daughter of John Caw, merchant, twice Lord Provost of Perth, and of Grace, eldest daughter of John McCall, of Belvedere House (now the Fever Hospital of Glasgow)   He received his early education at The Seminary, Perth.   When he was six months old he lost his father, and in 1845 his mother went to live in Edinburgh, and he attended the High School there.   At the age of fifteen he began his studies at the University of Edinburgh.   Having passed his examination for the Degree of M.D. a year before his age allowed him to graduate, he spent that time in the Schools of Paris, Vienna, Leipzig, etc.   After graduation in 1856 he had charge of Sir James Simpson's Ward in the Royal Infirmary, Edinburgh, for one year, and in 1857 became Junior Demonstrator to Professor Goodsir.   There being no prospect of promotion in Edinburgh, in 1861 Dr. Cleland accepted the position of Senior Demonstrator to Professor Allen Thomson, in the University of Glasgow.   In 1863 he was appointed by the Crown to the Chair of Anatomy and Physiology in Queen's College, Galway, where also he was one of the Clinical Teachers in Medicine and Surgery.

After holding the appointment in Galway for fourteen years, Dr Cleland returned to the University of Glasgow in 1877 as Regius Professor of Anatomy.

He married in 1888 the eldest daughter of John Hutton Balfour (who was from 1841 to 1845 Regius Professor of Botany in the University of Glasgow, and afterwards Professor of Botany in the University of Edinburgh, and Regius

Keeper of the Royal Botanic Gardens there for thirty-four years), and of Marion Spottiswood Bayley, daughter of Isaac Bayley, Esqr , S S C., of Manuel, Stirlingshire   Dr. Cleland has one son, born in 1889.

Children of William Cleland (112) and Mary Henderson.

ROBERT CLELAND (115) —Born 1831. Died in Queensland when a young man.

MARY CLELAND (116).—Unmarried.

JOHN WILLIAM HENDERSON CLELAND (117) —Born 1835. Major-General (retired) in H M. Indian Staff Corps. In compliance with testamentary instructions of his maternal uncle, he assumed, by Royal Licence, the additional surname of Henderson on succeeding to the property of Roke Manor in Hampshire.   He married, firstly, Isabella, daughter of M. Morphett (late Captain, 48th Regiment of Foot, a Peninsular officer), and by her had one son, John Macleod. He married, secondly, at the Cathedral, Bombay, in 1874, Charlotte Edith, 2nd daughter of Captain Fletcher F C. Hayes, M.A., 62nd Regiment (Military Secretary to Sir Henry Lawrence, of Lucknow, and only son of Commodore General Sir John Hayes, by his wife, Frances Henrietta, only daughter of General Robert Torrens, C B), and by her had three sons, Fletcher, William Charles, and Walter.

Captain Fletcher Hayes, during his short life, had a very distinguished career, both as a soldier and scholar   He could speak and correspond in eleven languages—Hindu, Urdu, Persian, etc.—and this knowledge was of much service officially in the various campaigns in which he took part. At the beginning of the Mutiny at Lucknow he volunteered for service on a dangerous and delicate mission; this was apparently successfully concluded, and he and his companion, Captain Carey, were returning to their escort, when they found that the men had mutinied and that Mr. Barber and Mr. Fayrer had been treacherously killed   In an endeavour to regain the British lines, Captain Hayes fell, but Captain Carey, who was further off, just successfully escaped. Captain Hayes matriculated at Magdalen College, Oxford, in 1847, passed the degree of B A. in 1849, and received that of M.A. in the same year.

WILLIAM CLELAND (118).—Colonel, now retired. Married in 1895, Minnie, daughter of — Julian Young, Esqr , by whom he has one daughter, born 1898. Served in India and Egypt.

JESSIE CLELAND (119).—Unmarried

CLELANDS OF THE 22nd GENERATION.

Children of Robert Cleland and Elizabeth Freeman.

JOHN RICHARD CLELAND (120).—Born in Canada, 1872, died 1874.

JANE KATHLEEN MARY CLELAND (121).—Born in the United States. Has studied singing in Paris and at the Royal Academy of Music, London.

LINDA HELEN CLELAND (122).—Born in Canada.

Children of John Cleland, F.R.S., and Ada Balfour.

JOHN ROBERT CLELAND (123).—Born in Glasgow, 4th November, 1889. Educated at Kelvinside Academy. A member of the Cadet Corps of his school, associated with the 4th V.B Scottish Rifles (Cameronian Regiment), which regiment was founded in 1689, chiefly through the efforts of William Cleland, its first Lieutenant-Colonel

Children of John William Henderson Cleland and Isabella Morphett.

JOHN MACLEOD CLELAND (124).—Born 1862. Married twice. No children by the first marriage; two daughters, Florence Edith, and Isabella (born 1903), by the second.

Children of John William Henderson Cleland and Edith Hayes.

FLETCHER HAYES CLELAND (125).—Born 1875 Married Zoe Wyndgate Higginson, daughter of Montague Higginson, Esqr., R.N , eldest son of the late Rev. — Higginson, formerly Vicar of Thormanley. Has two daughters, Betty Zoe Huband and Rachel Edith

WILLIAM CHARLES CLELAND.—Born, Trichinopoly, 1876, died 1877, at Conoor, Neilgherry Hills.

WALTER CLELAND.—Born 1878, in Switzerland. A lawyer now in Johannesburg, South Africa.

ROSE-CLELANDS OF COUNTY DOWN.

The following account is quoted in the "Herald and Genealogist" :—

Alexander Cleland, the twelfth Cleland of that ilk, married Mary, sister of John Hamilton, first Lord Bargany, and youngest daughter of Sir John Hamilton of Bargany and his spouse, Margaret Campbell, daughter of the Rev. (should it not be the *Right* Rev. ?) Alexander Campbell (Bishop of Brechin) of Ardkinlas, descended from Argyle. By her he had several sons, the eldest of whom sold the lands of Cleland to a cousin of his own name.

John Cleland (128) of Laird Braes, in the parish of Zeswalt (*sic.*? Leswalt), was either the second or the third son of the above Alexander Cleland, and was born about the year 1623 In consequence of some disagreement with his elder brother he retired in disgust to a small property, called "Laird Braes," in the parish of Zeswalt (*sic.*) and county of Wigton, and about the year 1651 married Katherine Ross, descended from the Rosses of Henning.* He died in 1683, leaving by his said wife his son and successor.

James Cleland (129) of Laird Braes, born in 1652, married in 1690 Agnes Innes, who was born in 1670, and descended from the Inneses of Benwall (?)† She died in 1711, and he died in 1717, leaving issue :—

John (130), born in 1692.

Mary (131), born in 1694, married James McEwan her third cousin, by whom she had a daughter and only child, born 8th October, 1728, married to Robert Innes, born in 1728, who died, s p 30th December, 1812.

The son and heir,

John Cleland of Whithorn, in Wigtonshire, Scotland, was appointed factor to James, fifth Earl of Galloway, and, in 1731, married Margaret Murdoch,‡ only child of Murdoch, Provost of Whithorn, descended from the Murdochs of Cumlodden, she was born in 1701, and died 21st September, 1747 ; he died 10th August, 1747, and had issue by her—

James (132), born 4th May, 1736 (of whom hereafter).

Agnes (133), born 4th September, 1740, married first at Fort St David's, in the East Indies, 5th June, 1766, to Lieut. Richard Rose, of the East India Company's European Regiment, who died at Trichinopoly, 7th June, 1768, of wounds received at the seige of Altoor, by whom she had an only child

James Dowsett Rose, who afterwards assumed the additional name of Cleland, born 24th March, 1767.

She married, secondly, in 1774, William Nicholson, Esq., of Ballow House, and died 11th July, 1775 (and was buried at Bangor, Ireland), without having issue by him.

The son and successor,

James Cleland, Esq , of Newtown Ards, co. Down, Ire-

* The respectable family of "Ross of Hayning Ross" owned lands prior to this period in the county of Ayr, and is no doubt the one here claimed as a relative, probably without warrant
† "Innes of Benwall " is doubtless imaginary.
‡ "Murdoch of Cumlodden " was a landed family, owning considerable property in the Stewartry of Kirkcudbright   Their estate of Cumlodden is now one of the seats of the Earl of Galloway , hence, perhaps, the idea of marrying his factor to a scion of the old proprietors.

land, married in 1770, Sarah, only child of Captain Patrick Baird (brother of William Baird of Newbyth, and James Baird, Esq., of London, and uncle to General Sir David Baird); he died at Newtown Ards, 14th May, 1777, s p. Will dated 5th May, 1775. His widow died and was buried at Abingdon, Berks, 7th December, 1787 Will dated 23rd November, 1787. Mr. Cleland was succeeded by his nephew, the present James Dowsett Rose-Cleland, Esq, of Rath-Gael

James Dowsett Cleland-Rose, Esq, of Rath-Gael House, co Down, born 24th March, 1767; succeeded his father 7th June, 1768, and to the property of his paternal grandfather, Richard Rose, Esq., of Abingdon, Berks, 14th January, 1784, and in compliance with the testamentary injunction of his cousin, Patrick Cleland, Esq., of Ballymagee, co. Down (to whose Irish estates he succeeded, 5th December, 1785), assumed the additional surname and arms of Cleland (his mother's name). His first wife having died without male issue surviving, he wedded, secondly, 10th December, 1832, Elizabeth, eldest daughter of William Nicholson Steel Nicholson, Esq, of Ballow House, and Elizabeth Hancock, his wife, and by her has two (three) other sons and a daughter (three daughters).

III.   James Blackwood, born 30th January, 1835.

IV.   Richard, born 1st May, 1836.   (This gentleman seems to be the present representative of the family.)

V.   Edward Allen, born 21st January, 1840.

I   Agnes Elizabeth   II.   Isabel Hamilton

III.   Margaret Sabina.

Mr. Rose Cleland is a magistrate and Deputy-Lieutenant for the county of Down. He commanded the Newtown Ards Yeomen Infantry at the battle of Saintfield, 9th June, 1798, in August following raised the Rath-Gael Yeomen Infantry, and received repeated thanks from the Government for his services, he also served the office of High Sheriff for the county of Down in 1805, and presided at the contested election for that county between Robert Stewart Viscount Castlereagh and Col. John Meade, which lasted twenty-one days.

Arms and supporters—which are those of the Old Clelands—

Azure, a hare salient argent with a hunting-horn round its neck vert, garnished gules, for Cleland, quartering Allen, Bennet, Murdoch, and Cleland. *(Burke's General Armoury)*

CRESTS.—A hawk on a left-hand glove proper, for Cleland. A rose gules, seeded and slipped proper, between two wings ermine, for Rose

Mottoes.—For sport; and Je pense a qui pense plus.

Supporters.—Two greyhounds proper collared or.

(The Herald and Genealogist, 1866.)

This genealogy is severely criticised in the "Herald and Genealogist," but as has been pointed out in dealing with the main line of the Clelands, we think unjustly. In the arms, however, the Rose-Clelands have adopted the Cleland supporters of two greyhounds, an act inexcusable, since the supporters can alone be carried by the head of the family, and the Rose-Clelands not only cannot claim such a position but are in fact only Clelands by the female side

The following additional information is gained from "Burke's Landed Gentry," 1894 :—

Gen. (e) James Dowsett Rose-Cleland, born 1767, died 1852.

Gen. (f) James Blackwood Rose-Cleland, born 1835, his son. Died in 1856. Succeeded by his brother.

Richard Rose-Cleland, born 1836, succeeded his brother 1856; married 1861, Elizabeth, daughter of Robert Kennedy, Esq , of Lisburn, co. Antrim. Died 1892, having had issue :—

Gen. (g)

I.   James Dowsett Rose-Cleland, born 1862.
II   Robert Kennedy Rose-Cleland, born 1863.
III.   Richard Rose-Cleland, born 1864, died 1865.
IV.   Charles Arthur, born 1876.
I   Elizabeth Helen Louisa.
II.   Mary Isabella Eveline.
III.   Edith Adelaide.
IV.   Maude Ethel.
V.   Florence May.
VI   Alice Gertrude.
VII.   Catherine Mabel.
VIII. Harriet Ella.

CLELANDS OF STORMONT CASTLE, CO. DOWN.

A County Down family, claiming descent from James Cleland of that ilk, co. Lanark.

REV JOHN CLELAND (134)—Prebendary of Armagh. Born 1755; married 1805 Esther, daughter and co-heiress of Samuel Jackson, of Stormont, by his wife, Margaret Vateau, of a Huguenot family. Died 1834, having had issue :—

I. SAMUEL JACKSON CLELAND (135), born 1808; married
Elizabeth Joyce in 1834; died 1842, leaving:

> 1. JOHN CLELAND (136), late of Stormont Castle.
> (See on.)
>
> 2. JAMES VANCE CLELAND (137), of Ennismore, co
> Armagh; born 1838; late Captain 3rd Hussars;
> married 1862, Emily, daughter of Sir George
> Molyneux, Bart; died 1886, leaving issue:
>> *(a)* SAMUEL (138), born 1864
>>
>> *(b)* GEORGE MOLYNEUX (139).
>
> 3. LT.-COL. ROBERT STEWART CLELAND (140).

" The third son of the late Samuel Cleland, Esq., of
Stormont Castle, and grandson of the Rev. John Cleland, Pre-
centor in the Cathedral of Armagh and Rector of Killevey.
. .   Born on the 24th June, 1840. Gazetted in 1857
to a cornetcy in the 7th Dragoon Guards . . . .
At the action of Killa Kazi on the 11th December (1878),
while gallantly leading the cavalry charge against overwhelm-
ing numbers of the enemy during the retirement, Colonel
Cleland was dangerously wounded. Becoming unconscious,
he was placed in a dhoolie, which was subsequently abandoned
by its bearers, with the guns, in a watercourse; he was, however, saved from the approaching enemy by the gallantry of
Sergeant-Major Young of the regiment, who, finding that he
did not reply when spoken to, dismounted, and dragged him
out of the litter into the water, the contact with which revived
him   The sergeant offered him his horse, which Colonel
Cleland refused. A few moments afterwards he managed to
seize the bridle of an animal galloping past with empty saddle,
and was assisted to mount   Ordering Young to collect and
lead the scattered men who were by this time coming up, and
taking a sergeant (Finn) to accompany him, he started for
Sherpur, eight miles distant. His elbow-joint had been shat-
tered by a sword-cut, and a bullet with which he had been
struck was still in his side. That he managed to reach the
cantonments over such country as lay before him, speaks of
itself for his heroic courage and endurance. . . . . At
Cabul he was most kindly and carefully treated . . . . by
his devoted friend, Captain Stewart Mackenzie . . . .
15th June, erysipelas appeared in his wounded arm. . . .
eventually died on the 7th August " *(Shadbolt's Afghan
Campaign, 1878-1880.)*

4. Samuel Frederick Stewart Cleland (141), born 1842
5. Margaret Cleland (142).

II. ROBERT STEWART CLELAND (143), born 1810; died under age.

III. SARAH FRANCES CLELAND (144); married 1831, Robert Richard Tighe; died 1832.

JOHN CLELAND (136), of Stormont Castle, co Down, born 1836; married 1859, Thérèse Maria, daughter of Captain Thomas Leyland, of Haggerston Castle, Northumberland. High Sheriff, 1866. Left issue:

1. ARTHUR CHARLES STEWART CLELAND (145), of Stormont Castle.
2. ANDREW LEYLAND HILLYAR CLELAND (146), born 1868.
3 FLORENCE RACHEL THERESE LAURA CLELAND (147); married, 1879, Edward Blachett, of Wylam, Northumberland

CLELANDS OF KNOWHOBLE HILL.

ORIGIN.—The first mention of a Cleland of Knohhobohill is in the testament of James Cleland of that ilk, who died in 1547, wherein he "ordanes and makis his son Arthur assignay in and to his stedying of Knokhobohill; and gif it failyeis of Arthure, as God forbid, I ordane my son Robene to have said stedying of Knokhobohill" *(Commis. Rec. Glasgow.)*

KNOWHOBLE HILL HOUSE —" Knowhoble Hill, a convenient dwelling, lying upon Teilling burn, with gardens well inclosed, belonging to Archbald Cleland." *(Hamilton of Wishaw, in 1710)*

" Their original residence was on a rocky eminence on the south bank of Tealing Burn, some of the old vaults being visible a few years ago." *(Grossart, 1880)*

" Upon the E.N E quarter (of the parish of Bothwell), there is a little rivulet called the Teeling Burn, which falls into the South Calder, a little above the house of Cleland. The burn runs much about a mile upon the borders of the Paroch, which it separates from that of Shotts The only thing remarkable upon it is the house of Connoblehill, in the paroch of Shotts—a family of the name of Cleland. It belongs to Captain William Cleland, one of the Commissioners in His Majestie's Navy." *(Geographical Description of Paroch of Bothwell. McFarlane MS S Probably by the incumbent, Mr. William Hamilton. Date about 1720)*

1st GENERATION.

RECORDS —The first of the family was ARTHUR (148), son of James, 10th of Cleland He was charged in 1572 as being guilty of treason. There was a marriage between Cleland of Knowenoblchill and a daughter of John Hamilton of Orbiston about the end of the sixteenth century. No name is given, but it was probably Arthur." *(Grossart, 1880.)*

2nd GENERATION.

WILLIAM CLELAND (149), OF KNOWHOBIHILL, a witness in 1608. Bought the lands of East and West Ballinbreich from James Tolwart in the same year   Mentioned in a deed, 1612. *(Reg. Great Seal)*

In 1608 James Ros of Wardlaw is surety for 1,000 merks for William Cleland of Konnoblehill, not to harm John Turnble, etc. He appears as a complainer in 1612. *(Reg. Privy Council)*

His brother JOHN CLELAND (150), Shoemaker, Burgess of Edinburgh, mentioned in 1593, 1614   *(Reg Great Seal.)*

"Test &c Wm. Cleland of Knowhobihill quha deceist in pe moneth of July, 1615," &c "Legacie   .   The said Wm being seik in bodie, &c , nominat, &c Troyalus Eistorm . . . . his only Exr. . . . mairovir, the said Wm Cleland nominati, &c. James Cleland of that-Ilk, John Cleland, burges of Edt broper to pe said Williame, &c. tutouris to Johne, James, Andro and Grissall, his lawt full bairnes, q^u p^r perfyte aiges rex^{tine} and to have pe administratune of pe landis, roumes, &c " *(Conf Dec 7, 1615.)*

He was succeeded by his eldest son, William.

3rd GENERATION

WILLIAM CLELAND (151).—"Margaret Baillie, spous to William Cleland of Knowhobilhill," deceased October, 1630. The inventory of her effects is " gevin up be the said William Cleland, hir spous, In name and behalf of Williame, James. Elizabethe, Jeane, Jonet, and Grissel Clelandis, thair law^t-full bairnes" &c —Conf. March 9 following————William Cleland yor of Knowhobilhill appears April, 1651. *(Comm. Rec. Glasgow, quoted by Hamilton of Wishaw in " Sheriffdoms of Lanark and Renfrew." 1710)* In 1627, William Cleland, of Konnoblehill, is one of the custodians of James Cleland, younger, of Faskine. *(Reg Great Seal.)* " In 1640, William Cleland of Knoweno'lchill, was an clder

in Shotts congregation, and in 1648 he took part in the
'Unlawful Engagement,' for which he had to do penance before the congregation. *(Grossart.)*

4th GENERATION.

WILLIAM CLELAND (152), OF CONNOBLEHILL.—Appears
in 1651 as "younger," above. "William Cleland fear
of Knowhobillhill" appears in 1656; in 1659 he
appears again in a bond written by "Archibald Cleland,
sone to William Cleland fier of Connoblehill," and witnessed
by "William Cleland, elder of Connobilhill, and Archibald
Cleland, writer hereof"; in 1675 "William Cleland of Connoblehill" occurs again as having been "cautioner to John
Cleland in Overtoune of Cambusnethan, and failzieing him be
deceis to Kathareine Cleland his dochter," in 1646; William
and Archibald Cleland of Connoblehill occur again in 1673.
(Comm. Glasgow)

JAMES CLELAND (153), brother. "Son to umqll William
Cleland of Knowhobellhill," in 1693. In 1697 in the Session
Records.

ELIZABETH, JEAN, JANET, GRISSEL, sisters.

About the middle of the seventeenth century (about 1675.—
J.B.C.) Cleland of Knowenoblehill married Ann, daughter of Gavin
Hamilton, of Raploch *(Grossart.)* "Cleland of Howhoble-
hun" is fined £600 in 1662. *(Thomson's Acts.)* This was
one of the fines imposed by Middleton in the Parliament of
1662 on those excepted from the Act of Indemnity *(Wodrow.)*
In the Session Records for 1652 appears a John Cleland of
Knowenoblehill. *(Grossart)*

5th GENERATION.

ARCHIBALD CLELAND (154) OF CONNOBLEHILL.—Living
at Connoblehill in 1710 *(Hamilton of Wishaw.)* Appears
in the Laing Charters in 1707. Elizabeth, spouse to
Archibald Cleland, younger, of Knownoblehill, appears in a
test conf, 27th October, 1666 "Archibald Cleland of Connobilhill" appears in a bond in the Commiss. of Glasgow in
1684, "Archibald Clelland of Knowhoblehill," with "Mr.
Gavin and Archibald Clelands, my sons," as witnesses, in
1698. In the same Commissariat, "Mr. Joseph Cleland in
Knohobillhill, and James Cleland, his brother-germane,"
appear in 1691; the former is probably the "Mr. Joseph
Cleland, Minister at Dalscoff," married to Mary Muirhead,
mentioned in 1687. He distinguished himself in 1683 by his
diligence in giving informations. *(Wodrow.)*

6th GENERATION.

Gavin Cleland (155) —Mentioned above.

Archibald Cleland (156).—Mentioned above.

Captain William Cleland (157) —Owning Connoblehill in 1720, is probably the son of Archibald Cleland, 5th of Connoblehill, and is perhaps the same person as the Captain William Cleland living at Auchinlea in 1731. If this is so, the Clelands of Auchenlea may be considered as the representatives of those of Connoblehill This Captain William Cleland is styled " of Konnoblehill and Tapeley, Devonshire," in " Notes and Queries " " The Clelands were in possession of Knowenoblehill till the beginning of the present century." *(Grossart, 1880)*

CLELANDS OF AUCHINLEA.

Auchinlea is now occupied by large works. It is about a mile from Cleland ; what was pointed out to me as " Auchinlea House" was a newish-looking building. Auchinlea Farm, which belongs to a Grant, and has done so for many generations, stands further back from the road. *(Notes, 1903)*

Grossart says of this family :—" I do not meet with any authentic account of Cleland of Auchenlee till about the beginning of the seventeenth cvntury (? mistake for eighteenth century). It is usually stated, that when Alexander Cleland sold the estate of Cleland (Grossart refers to the second sale in 1711) he reserved Auchenlee, but it has already been shown that all the reservation he made was the feu-ferm rights of Little Hareshaw, and this branch must have been established a century before the sale of Cleland estate " (In 1711)

This branch of the family arrogated to themselves—in later days, at any rate—the chiefship of the name, using the supporters to the coat-of-arms. It was apparently the representative of this branch—who styled themselves " Cleland of Cleland and Auchinlea "—whose carriage coat-of-arms was the object of ire to the Cleland of that ilk of the 18th generation, when he seized the passing painter's brush in Princes Street and deleted the supporters. Silver-plate in their possession bore the supporters, and copies of the coat-of-arms with supporters appear in books owned by Dr. William Cleland (of Auchinlea), who graduated M.D. at Leyden in 1776.

I think it possible that the Clelands of Auchinlea were a branch of, or the main stem of, those of Knownoblehill. This is based on the statement by William Hamilton, incumbent of Bothwell Parish, in 1720, that Captain Cleland, Commissioner of the Navy, lived in Knownoblehill at that date;

whereas in 1731, *et seq.*, we find him located at Auchinlea. Possibly during his father's lifetime he lived at Konnoblehill and on his death at Auchinlea.

1st GENERATION (on record).

WILLIAM CLELAND (158) lived at Auchinlee at the beginning of the century (eighteenth century, presumably). *(Grossart)* This I presume to be the man who married, according to a newspaper cutting of 1866, a Miss Robertson of Earnoch. This marriage will account for the relationship that the Commissioner of Customs points out exists between Dr. William Cullen (whose mother was a Miss Robertson of Earnoch) and Capt. Cleland, apparently this William's son.

2nd GENERATION.

CAPTAIN WILLIAM CLELAND (159), R N.—This is apparently the William Cleland who married Elizabeth Storie, a daughter of the Laird of Wester Braco, in Shotts parish. The first mention of Capt William Cleland, a Commissioner in the Navy, is in William Hamilton's "Description of Bothwell Parish" about 1720, where he describes Konnoblehill as belonging to him.

The following extracts are of interest. They show that this Captain Cleland, the ancestor of the Clelands of Auchinlea, was on good terms with Commissioner Cleland, the then recognised head of the family (as Nisbet states), and that they were relatives. A short description is also given of the voyage that Dr. Cullen took under the command of Capt. Cleland. The Auchinlea Clelands have always been proud of their connection with Dr Cullen, the famous physician, who, however, is said in later days not to have very well repaid their hospitality to him.

Extract from "Life of William Cullen, M D., Professor of the Practice of Physic in the University of Edinburgh," by John Thomson. M D , etc., Professor of Medicine, and General Pathology in the University of Edin 1st Ed., 1828, second edition, 1859

"Dr Cullen was born at Hamilton on the 15th day of April, 1710. His father, who was a writer or attorney by profession and factor to the Duke of Hamilton, was proprietor of a small estate in the adjoining parish of Bothwell, which had been in the possession of his ancestors for many generations. His mother was a daughter of Mr Robertson of Whistleberry, a younger son of the family of Robertson of Earnock . . . On finishing his medical studies at Glasgow, Dr Cullen went to London, towards the end of the year 1729, with the view of obtaining a situation in which he might enjoy opportunities of acquiring a practical knowledge of his profession. Soon after arriving there, he had the good fortune to be appointed surgeon to a merchant ship, the Captain of which, Mr Cleland, of Auchinlea, was a relation of his own His appointment to this situation is mentioned in the following passage of a letter from his eldest brother to his mother, dated Edinburgh, 9th December, 1729 'Mr Hamilton, of Dalserf, got a letter last day from London from his brother Alexander, wherein he tells him that he was present with Captain Cleland when Commissioner Cleland* solicited him very strongly in favour of one Mr Cullen, a son of Saughs, and used very strong arguments with him to take care of him; and among the rest, that he was a cousin of the Captain's.' So the Captain promised to provide for him; but William desires that Dalserf would write to the Captain and thank him for it, for he said it was much owing to his letter I assure you everybody thinks my brother very lucky; for Mr. Alexander writes also that the Captain has had a levee, like a General's, every day; and there have been many solicitations for that very appointment "

" The vessel to which Dr. Cullen was appointed surgeon, was engaged in trading to the Spanish Settlements in the West Indies, and remained during her voyage for six months at Porto Bello.
Dr Cullen returned to Scotland in the end of the year 1731, or in the beginning of 1732. His eldest brother having died during his absence, the duty devolved upon him of arranging his father's affairs and of providing, as far as was in his power, for the education and settlement of his younger brothers and sisters In these circumstances he was invited by his friend Captain Cleland to reside with him at his family estate of Auchinlea, in the parish of Shotts, and to take charge of the health of his son who was affected with a lingering disorder. This situation was peculiarly convenient for Dr Cullen in commencing the practice of his profession. It was near to Hamilton, the place of his birth, and in the vicinity of the residences of many of the most considerable families in the County of Lanark. It was in the neighbourhood also of his patrimonial property, the lands of Saughs and of another small farm which belonged to his family in the parish of Shotts Whilst residing there he seems to have combined with his medical practice the most unremitting application to his studies Captain Cleland was often heard to say that nothing could exceed his assiduity at this period, for when not engaged visiting patients, or in preparing medicines for them, his time was wholly occupied with his books."

Extract from " Discourses on Philosophy," etc., by Sir William Hamilton, Bart , 1853, " On the Revolutions of Medicine in reference to Cullen "
" William Cullen was born at Hamilton in the year 1710. By his father, a writer (Anglice, attorney) by profession and factor to the

---

* The friend of Mr Pope and author of a letter prefixed to the Dunciad in the edition of Pope's works, printed at Edinburgh in 1767, Vol III.

Duke of Hamilton, he was sprung from a respectable line of ancestors, who had for several generations been proprietors of Saughs, a small estate in the parish of Bothwell; through his mother, he was descended from one of the most ancient families in the County of Lanark, the Robertsons of Earnock.   . .

. . . . . Having exhausted the opportunities of improvement which Glasgow supplied, Cullen, with the view of obtaining a professional appointment went in his twentieth year to London. Through the interest of Commissioner Cleland (Will Honeycomb of the ' Spectator '), probably his kinsman, he was appointed to a merchant vessel trading to the Spanish Settlement in the West Indies, commanded by Captain Cleland of Auchinlea, a relation of his own. In this voyage he remained for six months at Porto Bello, thus enjoying an opportunity of studying the effects of a tropical climate on the constitution. . . . Two years, 1732-1734, he spent in the family of Captain Cleland, at Auchinlea in the Parish of Shotts, wholly occupied in the study and occasional practise of his profession "

" Elizabeth eldest daughter of a Capt. Wm. Cleland, R N., married Sir William Johnston of that ilk, sixth baronet being his second wife He succeeded in 1750 There were three sons William, his apparent heir, John, Alexander; and three daughters, Elizabeth, Mary Selby and Jean Charlotte " *(Burke)*

A newspaper cutting of 1866 gives James, Andrew, John, Mary, Jennet and Christina as being the names of the children of William Cleland and Elizabeth Storie Possibly some of these are not so, but children of Dr. Wm Cleland, their grandson. There is no mention of an Elizabeth, for instance, yet she has her mother's name.

In Charnoth's ' Naval Biography ' is mentioned a *Captain John Cleland. A Captain William Cleland* appears to have died in the Mediterranean, May 18th, 1743.

Captain William Cleland, R N , of Queen Street, Westminster, and of Essex, " representative of the ancient family of Cleland of that ilk," appears in the Scots Magazine (notice of Lady Johnstoune's death). His daughters were —1 Elizabeth, died August 25, 1772, having married March 10th, 1757, Sir William Johnstone, Bart , and had issue; 2 Margaret, died May 6, 1810, aet seventy-eight, having married Rev. A. Uvedale, Rector of Barking, Essex, and had issue. *(Gent Magazine, " Notes and Queries.")*

These two references to Capt. William Cleland must, I feel sure, refer to Capt William Cleland of Auchinlea; his being styled " representative of the ancient family of Cleland of that ilk " strengthens this conviction, since the Clelands of Auchinlea have always prided themselves on a close connection with the main stem. The mention of the two daughters, Elizabeth and Margaret, neither of whom appear in the newspaper cutting of 1866, as being children of " William Cleland and Elizabeth Storie," makes it uncertain whether Capt. William

Cleland married Elizabeth Storie or Miss Robertson of Earnoch, or whether there is here a hopeless mixture of names and generations.

The will of "William Cleland of Auchinlea" was confirmed 27th March, 1749. *(Commiss. of Glasgow.)*

3rd GENERATION.

(1) JAMES CLELAND (160) of Auchinlea —"William Cleland, who married Elizabeth Storie, must have died before 1742, as in that year his widow and eldest son, James, let in lease the mailing of North Meikle Hareshaw to Margaret Brownlee, relict of George Cleland of South Shaws. James is said to have sold Auchinlea to Robert Carrick of Braco He was paying Cess in 1797 for the lands of Auchenlee, North Shaws, Fernieshaw, and North Meikle Hareshaw. One of the witnesses to the above lease was William Cleland of Langbyers and was probably a son of William (*i.e*, James' father; this is apparently incorrect). He (presumably James) was married to Catherine Cameron, daughter of William Cameron, minister at Greenock Mrs. Cameron made her will in 1722, leaving her daughter, Mrs. Cleland, a legacy of five hundred merks " *(Grossart.)*

The lands of Auchenlee were sold by James Cleland, first son (of William, who married Elizabeth Storie), 1808, to Robert Carrick, banker, Glasgow. *(Newspaper Cutting, 1866)* (Note —There is an inconsistency here : if James Cleland, as Grossart asserts, was married in 1722, he must have been about 20 then at most; in 1808 he would be 106 years old. Grossart may have made a mistake in the date 1722, or Catherine Cameron may have been the wife of William Cleland of Langbyers)

(2) ANDREW CLELAND (161).—Brother.

(3) JOHN CLELAND (162) —Brother. Married Mary Wardrop, daughter of the Laird of Forestburn (parish of Shotts) ; was farmer in Langbyers and Langbridge, both in the parish of Shotts ; afterwards purchased the lands of Ravenshall. From him were descended William, Betsy, Peggy, James, Barbara, John, and Mary Cleland.

(4) MARY CLELAND (163) —Sister.

(5) JENNET CLELAND (164).—Sister.

(6) CHRISTINA CLELAND (165) —Sister.

4th GENERATION.

(1) WILLIAM CLELAND, M.D. (166).—Born about 1750. Eldest son of James Cleland of Auchenlee.

" Dissertatio medica inauguralis,
de
Variolarum Insitione,
quam,
Nicolai Hoogoliet,
S S Theolog Doct ejusdemque facultatis in Academia Lugduno Batava
Professoris Ordinarii, verbi divini in eadem urbe ministri,
nec non
Amplissimi Senatus Academici Consensu, &
Nobilissimae Facultatis Medicae Decreto
Pio giadu Doctoratus
Summisque in Medicina Honoribus ac Privilegiis, rite ac
legitime consequendis,
Eruditorum Examini subjicit
Gulielmus Cleland
Scoto-Britannicus
Ad diem X. Maji, hora undecima L S

Lugduni Batavorum.
Apud Jacobum Murray   1776."

The thesis is dedicated to " Patri optimo, jure venerando, Jacobo Cleland, Scotiæ armigero, to Alexander Low, and to Dr. William Cullen, the physician "

The above dissertation on inoculation for smallpox was presented by Dr. William Cleland to the University of Leyden in 1776   I have seen two copies of it—one in the Collection of William Hunter's books in the Glasgow University, the other in the Library of Dr. Cleland, Professor of Anatomy there (1903).   The latter copy has affixed to it a coat-of-arms containing the principal arms of the Clelands of Cleland with supporters.   Whether the assumption of these arms was based on a claim to be head of the family (who only is entitled to supporters), or whether the supporters were assumed in ignorance of their import, I do not know.

This is probably the Dr Cleland whom William, son of Walter, and William, son of Robert, met at or near Lanark when they made an excursion thither in search of remnants of the family.   This would probably be between 1810 and 1830.   (If Dr Cleland were 21 when he presented his thesis in 1776, he would be about 55 in 1810, and 75 in 1830.   After graduating he would probably return to his home in Lanarkshire, and we are unlikely to find two Dr Clelands alive there at the same time in those days.) This Dr. Cleland gave William, the son of Walter, in acknowledgment of his being the head of the family, an old snuff mull with the crest on it. Professor Cleland, F R S., thinks this man must be Miss Steel's uncle

Professor Cleland appends this note to his copy of Dr. William Cleland's thesis.—"This Dr. William Cleland was perhaps uncle to Miss Steel, whose mother was a Miss Cleland of Auchinlee, and who states that her uncle, Dr. Cleland, was the last of the old family. But there is evidence that the sale of the estates to a 'cousin of the same name' spoken of in Nisbet's Heraldry really took place. The supporters were assumed illegally by the family, who for a while came into possession; and doubtless it was an Auchinlee man—possibly this Dr. Cleland's father, from the panels of whose carriage my great-grandfather deleted the supporters with a brush taken from the pot of a painter who happened to be passing in Princes Street, Edinburgh." *(J Cleland)*

What relationship this man bore to the direct line of Cleland of Cleland I cannot discover, but I think there is little doubt that this is the Dr. Cleland who acknowledged William, son of Walter, to be the chief of the family, convinced by evidence brought forward by William.

This Dr William Cleland is mentioned again in 1813. A meeting of heritors of the parish of Shotts was called at this date to put a stop to burying within the walls of the Parish Church, and Dr. Cleland writes a letter to them "protesting against any resolution that may affect my very ancient privilege of burying within the walls of the present Kirk." This Dr Cleland's daughter, Christina apparently, married a Mr. Robert Craig; his grand-daughter, Miss Craig, married a Mr. Thomson; and of two great-grand-daughters, Miss Thompsons, one married Sir Douglas Maclagan, the surgeon, the other Mr Scott.

(2) A sister of Dr. William Cleland, who married Alexander Low, stated in Dr Cleland's thesis to be "mercator sagassimus apud Rotterdamensis, sororis maritus, amicus suus."

(3) WILLIAM (167), son of John Cleland of the 3rd generation, surgeon, Stonehouse, born 30th October, 1766, married Agnes Bell, daughter of Robert Bell, merchant in St. Andrew's, by whom were descended John, Robert, Agnes, James, Mary, Betsy, William, Margaret, and Mary Cleland.

(4) JOHN (168), son of John Cleland, married in 1806 to Isabella Bell, daughter of Thomas Bell of Westerhouse, in

Carluke parish, and was farmer at Limig   Part of the family by this marriage still reside in Shotts parish. *(Grossart)*

(5) JAMES (169), son of John Cleland, married to Elizabeth Mack   He was proprietor of Ravenshall, and had a lease of Langbyers.

(5) ROBERT (170), son of John Cleland, died unmarried.

5th GENERATION.

Daughter of Dr. William Cleland, son of James Cleland.

(1) Daughter married Robert Craig.

Children of William, son of John Cleland :

(1) John Cleland (171)
(2) Agnes Cleland
(3) James Cleland (172).
(4) Robert Cleland (173), third son, born 11th March, 1799, married Robina, second daughter of Henry Redpath, clock and watchmaker, Stirling.
(5) Mary Cleland.
(6) Betsy Cleland
(7) William Cleland (174).
(8) Margaret Cleland.
(9) Mary Cleland.

Children of John, son of John Cleland.

Resided in Shotts parish.

Dr. William Cleland, leaving no male heirs, his daughter, Mrs. Craig, hearing that a Mr. Cleland, a railway station-master in Ireland, claimed to be head of the Auchinlea branch, before her death sent to him a snuff box with the Cleland arms upon it

(NOTE —In a newspaper cutting for 1866, descent is claimed for the Clelands of Auchinlea from the son of Alexander of that ilk, who sold the estate about 1640   This son was born about *1620* . in this genealogy he is called " William Cleland, who married Miss Robertson, of Earnoch," and his *grandson,* a James Cleland, is said to have sold Auchinlea in *1808.* It is, of course, practically impossible that a grandfather born in 1620 would have a grandson alive in 1808, 188 years later   Possibly the William Cleland who married Miss Robertson may have been a son of the Alexander Cleland, self-styled of that ilk, who about 1680 married Margaret Hamilton, of Wishaw, and about 1707 himself re-sold the estate   Even this leaves still a long gap.   Curiously enough this genealogy is prefixed by an account taken from Nisbet's Heraldry, wherein Major William Cleland is styled the head of the family and a great-grandson of Alexander Cleland, yet no mention of him occurs in the Auchinlea additions.)

CLELANDS OF FASKINE.

ORIGIN.—"From James Cleland of that ilk, who in the reign of James III. married Jean, daughter of William Lord Somerville (as in the manuscript of that family), branched Cleland of Faskine, Cleland of Monkland, and Cleland of Gartness " *(Nisbet's Heraldry, 1722. Corrected.)*

ARMS.—Cleland of Faskine carries as above (*i e.*, the principal arms of the family), with the addition of a "Chief, Argent, charged with a sword fesse-ways, Azure; hilted and pomelled, Or (Lion Register)." *(Nisbet's Heraldry, 1722.)*

William Cleland of Faskine records, about 1685, in the Lyon Register :—" Azure, a hare salient argent, with a hunting horn about his neck, gules, garnished and stringed, or, on a chief of the second a sword fesseways, hilted and pomelled of the fourth, crest, a falcon rising proper, motto, *Si Pouvois.*"

FASKINE HOUSE —" Upward upon the water of Calder, in this old parish (*i e.*, Monkland), is Faskine, which long appertained to the Clelands; a pleasant seat, fyne wood and good gardens It belongs now to Dr. Wm. Wright, physician " *(Hamilton of Wishaw, 1710.)*

1st GENERATION.

——— CLELAND (175) of Faskine, brother to William Cleland, 8th of that ilk. Born about 1452.

2nd GENERATION.

WILLIAM CLELAND (176) of Faskine, and his cousin, Alexander Cleland, 9th of that ilk, " were both killed fighting valiantly for their King in the fatal battle of Flowden, 1513 " *(Nisbet)* Married Margaret Hamilton.

3rd GENERATION.

(1) JOHN CLELAND (177) of Faskine. Married Agnes Muirhead. Mentioned from 1531-1589.

In 1531 he acquired the feufirm rights of some lands in Bakrow for himself and his heirs, etc., "from the King." *(Reg of the Great Seal of Scotland. Vol. 1513-1546, No 1074.)* In 1543 he resigns these lands, which had been given him in James V.'s reign *(Idem No. 2935)* On the 2nd December of the same year, at Edinburgh, he appears as cautioner, signing himself thus, "Johnne Cleland of Foskane, with my hand at the pen " *(Reg of Privy Council of Scotland, Vol. 1)* On 8th September, 1571, "Joanni Kneland de Foskane, Oswaldo K., Gavino K , Georgo K., ejus fratribus," are amongst those to whom the king " remisit rancorem animi sui, sectam regiam et omnem actionum pro eorum proditoria existentia contra regem ad campum seu bellum de Langsyde," etc., which shows that he and his brothers were partisans of Queen Mary. This may account for the feuds and troubles we find some of them are mixed up with later. *(Reg. of Great Seal, Vol 1546-1580, No 1969)* In 1565 he is mentioned in the " Remission to the Duke of Chatelherault." (See Cleland of that ilk) In 1579, mentioned again *(Reg of Privy Council, Vol. III.)* In 1584, mentioned in the marriage contract of his daughter Janet. *(Renwick's "Glasgow Protocols.")* Alive in 1589, since his son John is then styled "younger of Faskine "

(b) OSWALD CLELAND (178), brother of John Cleland of Faskine Married Elizabeth Muirhead. 1554, witness to a charter of Adam Boyd. *(Reg of Great Seal. Vol. 1546-1580, No. 942.)* Mentioned in 1571 as above, as a follower of Queen Mary. Evidently died before 1582, as in that year his widow is mentioned. *(Renwick's "Glasgow Protocols," Vol. VIII., No 2441.)*

(c) GAVIN CLELAND (179).—Later of Gartscherie, brother of John Cleland of Faskine.

In 1532 and 1539 witness to charters. *(Reg. Great Seal, Vol. 1513-1546, Nos. 1197, 2111)* In 1551, " Regina, etc , dedit literas legitimationis Johanni Cleland bastardo, filio naturale Gavini C." *(Idem., Vol 1546-1580, No 655.)* In 1571 he is granted a remission for having sided with Queen Mary, as above. In 1576 the King confirmed a charter of John, Archbishop of St Andrew's, to Gavin Cleland of the lands of Gartscherie, for himself and his heirs, signed in 1565 ; his heirs failing, to go to James Kneland, second son of John Kneland of Foscan. *(Reg of Great Seal, Vol 1546-1580, No. 2568)*

Mentioned in the remission to the Duke of Chatelherault, 1565. On 27th April, 1568, mentioned as a rebel, thus :

" The quhilk day Johnne Hammiltoun of Stanehous, Sherefdepute of the Sherefdome of Lanark, being callit in presens of my Lord Regentis Grace and Lordis of Secret Counsall, to answer and gif declarationis, upoun the diligence writ and done by him in serchering, seking, taking and apprehending of *Gavin Cleland. Margaret Hammiltoun his moder*, Cuthbert Craig and James Wod in Gartschary, denunceit rebellis and put to the horne, be verted of lettres in the four formes, past upoun ane decreit in the Lordis of Counsall and Sessioun at the instance of Alexander Hume, son laawful to Johnne Hume of Coldenknowis, Knight for now removing, desisting and ceissing fra the landis and steding of Gartscharye, leasid in the barony of Monkland, within the Sherefdome of Lanark." *(Reg. of Privy Council, Vol. 1.)*

Between 1569 and 1578, he and others are cited for assault, thus :—

"Gavin Cleland engaged with Hamiltoun of Aihenheid and several other Hamiltouns in attacking Walter Chapman and his servant with daggis, battownis, and great endis of speris, and leaving him for deid, plundering his farm, etc , they are all declared rebell and at the horne, ordered to be apprehended and taken before the Lord Regent at Edinburgh that they may be punished." *(Idem , Vol II)*

(d) GEORGE CLELAND (180), brother of John Cleland of Faskine Probably George Cleland of Glenhuif, who married Margaret Hamilton. *(See Clelands of Glenhuif.)*

4th GENERATION.

(a) JOHN CLELAND (181) of Faskine, son of John Cleland of Faskine. Married Jean Creichton In 1580, 1589, mentioned as being younger of Faskine *(Reg. of Great Seal.)*

In 1595 is mentioned (with his wife) as still "fiar." *(Glasgow Protocols.)* In 1599, mentioned with his wife, Jean Creichton, as giving sasine. *(Renwick's Glasgow Protocols)* In 1600, mentioned in connection with the marriage contract of his sister, Christina. *(Idem.)* In 1603, John Cleland of Foskane, and Jean Creychton, his wife, and the lands of Foskane, are mentioned; he is not to reset or intercommune with Adame Boyd, son of Lord Boyd, during his rebellion. *(Reg Privy Council)* In the same year he is surety for Robert Boyd of Badinhaith. John Cleland of Foskane is on the Commission for the Peace, Lanarkshire, in 1612, 1614, and 1623. *(Reg. Privy Council.)*

(b) JAMES CLELAND (182) of Monkland, second son of John Cleland of Faskine and Agnes Muirhead. *(See Monkland Branch)*

(c) ROBERT CLELAND (183), burgess of Glasgow. Mentioned about 1590 with others for arson, thus :—

"Complaint by Dame Dorathie Stewart, Countess of Gowrie, and Issobell Hume, relict of Thomas Cranstoun, fiar of Crosbie, that Robert Cleland and others to the number of 100 persons went to his complainers lands of Teithheid quhais maliciously they rased fyre and brint and distroyit ane grite quantitie of turffis." *(Reg of Privy Council, Vol IV.)*

November, 1607, mentioned as owning "duo tenement terrarum in burgo de Rutherglen et 15 denariatas terrarum in Spittel-quarter." *(Reg. Great Seal)*

Robert Cleland, merchant in Glasgow, bought the manse of the Rector of Stobo in Glasgow, from whom, in 1649, it was transmitted to Agnes Cleland, daughter of George Cleland in Glenhuiff, and John Cleland her husband *(Glasgow Protocols.)* The manse seems to have passed from Robert's hands to his elder brother, James ; from him to his brother, John Cleland of Foskane, who disposed of it to George Cleland, and the latter to Agnes, his daughter. *(Reg. Great Seal)*

In 1606, Robert Cleland appears in the Register of the Privy Council :—

" Sir George Elphinstoun of Blythswode, provost, and the Bailies and Council of Glasgow complain against Sir Matthew Stewart of Minto, Sir Walter Stewart his son and a number of the citizens and craftsmen of Glasgow for organised riot in opposition to certain changes promoted by the complainers in the matter of the election of the Magistrates of the City. *Robert Cleland* is one of the number who ' maist factienshe and seditiouslie convocat and assembled togidder ' "

He is mentioned in the same complaint as being one of " a grite number of airmed men of the seditious faction of the citie " who " attendit upon the said Laird of Mynto " and " maid onsett on " the Lord Provost

" Charge is given to the whole party to appear *(Robert Cleland* being one of them) and answer. The Laird of Mynto and a certain number are found guilty and ordered to be confined in the burgh of Linlithgow till his Majesty's will be known. The remaining number, of whom *Robert Cleland* appears to have been one, were assoilzied from all parts of the complaint and allowed to depart home at their pleasure "

Robert Cleland, burgess of Glasgow, brother of the guidman of Foscane, occurs in the testament of " Elizabeth Hamiltone, sister-germane to John Hamiltone of Grainge, besyde Kilmarnock," June, 1611.

(d) GEORGE CLELAND (184) and JAMES CLELAND (185), brothers of John Cleland of Faskine, occur in 1599 in the Register of the Privy Council, thus :—

Complaint by James Craufurde, brother of the bailie of Monkland. " Upon 10th July instant James and George Clelandis, brothers of Johnne Cleland of Foscane by special direction of said Johnne, cam furth of his dwelling house Foscan to the lande of Dundynen " they houghed a horse and returned to Foscan where they were resetted by their said brother.

Johnne appeared personally and was remitted by the Lords to the Judge ordinary and to find caution in £1,000 that he " shall underlie the law before the justice " James and George failing to appear were denounced rebels.

(d) ALEXANDER CLELAND (186), mentioned below.

(e) JANET CLELAND (187), married Alexander Baillie. The marriage settlement, signed by her father, is drawn up in 1584 *(Glasgow Protocols.)*

(f) CHRISTINA "CLEYLAND" (188) married George Anderson. Their marriage contract, drawn up in 1600, is signed by her brothers, John Cleland of Faskine and Alexander.

5th GENERATION.

JAMES CLELAND (189) OF FASKINE, son of John Cleland of Faskine.

James Cleland is mentioned in 1627 in the curious sale of the lands of Faskine to him by his father, with consent of his uncle, Sir James Cleland of Monkland, William Cleland of Konnoblehill (a distant cousin), and George Cleland of Glenhuiff (his cousin).

Apud Halyrindhous, 30 Jul. 1631. Rex—cum consensu, etc.—confirmat cartam quondam Joannis Cleland de Foscane,—qua, pro perimpletione contractus inter se ab una, et Jac. C. filium suum primogenitum et heredem apparentem, cum consensu D. Jacobi Cleland de Monkland militis, Gulielmi Cleland de Knohobillhill, Jacobi Hamiltoun de Hill, Jacobi Muirhead de Braiddinsholme et Georgii Cleland de Glenhuiff ejus curatorum, ab altera partibus, de data presentium,—vendidit dicto Jacobo Cleland (postea de Foscane) filio suo, et heredibus masc. ejus de corpore legitime procreandis, quibus deficientibus, ejus heredibus masculis et assignatis quibuscunque,—ter. de Foscane," etc Apud Foscane, 2 Jun. 1627 *(Reg Great Seal)*

In 1641, James Cleland of Faskine sells to John Moir of Shawheid that part of Faskine called Cairnhill. *(Idem.)* In 1642 and 1654 he appears in the Com. Rec. of Glasgow. "James Cleland of Faskine: act and decreet against him, 1661." *(Thomson's Acts of Scotch Parliament)* In "ane roole of the Heritors names of Monkland and Calder" in Munim. Univ. Glasg., dated 1659, appears, "Foscan, 7 lib. land   James Cleland, heritor." The will of James Cleland of Faskine, parish of Old Monkland, is confirmed June, 1670. *(Comm. of Hamilton and Campsie.)*

6th GENERATION.

(a) JAMES CLELAND (190) of Faskine.

In 1675, James Cleland of Faskine is named heir of his father, James Cleland of Faskine. *(Inquisitionem ad Gapellum Domini Regi Retornatarum.)*   In 1676, "the deceased

James Cleland, elder, of Faskine, and James Cleland, younger feir theirof,' are mentioned. *(Comm. Glasgow.)*

(b) In 1678, WILLIAM CLELAND (191) OF FASKINE is named heir of his brother James. *(Idem.)* "William Cleiveland," in "Acts of Privy Council," 14th May, 1678, is appointed lieutenant of a troop of Dragoons   Commissioner of Supply for Lanark, 1685. *(Thomson.)*

Captain William Cleland is mentioned in "Wodrow" as being an officer in the Royal Army, opposed to Argyle in his rebellion of 1685, and was killed in a skirmish at Muirdyke by Sir John Cochrane. *(See "Memoirs of Veitch," p. 328)*

Commission by the lords of his Majesty's Privy Council to various persons to search for and bring to trial heritors and others suspected guilty of rebellion. Commissioner for Clydesdale, Captain William Cleland of Foscane, 1683. His troop sent to Ayrshire, 1684, 80 prisoners carried from Dumfries to Peebles under a guard of three troops of dragoons, commanded by Captain Cleland, 1684. *(Wodrow.)*

(c) ALEXANDER CLELAND (192), of Dormonsyde, brother germane of William Cleland of Faskine

7th GENERATION.

JOHN CLELAND (193) of Faskine, son of Alexander Cleland, is named heir to William Cleland of Faskine in 1686   *(Inquisitionem, etc)* Forfeited for rebellion with Viscount Dundee, 1690. *(Thomson.)*

"This family terminated in an heir female " *(Appended to extract from Nisbet's Heraldry, written in 1800.)*

CLELANDS OF MONKLAND AND GARTNESS.

ORIGIN.—" From James Cleland (not William Cleland, as Nisbet says) of that ilk, in the reign of James III , branched Cleland of Monkland " *(Nisbet, 1722.)*

MONKLAND HOUSE —" The place of Monkland is first to be considered. Which was a large bodie of a house, with two jambs and four rounds, built by Sir James Cleland of Monkland, upon the lands of Peddersburne ; and was repute the best contrived house in all that neighbourhood. .   . It belongs to William Hamilton of Monkland, grandchild to Hamilton of Dalzell   The land, with the teinds of Monkland and Calder, was purchased from Sir James sone by the Duke of Hamilton , and sold by the Duchess, the lands to James Hamilton of Dalzell, and the teinds to the colledge of Glasgow." *(Hamilton of Wishau, 1710.)*

"About a large half mile north from Lachop, upon the north lip of the water, and within the paroch of New Monkland, stands the house of Monkland. This formerly belonged to Sir James Cleland, who built a very large house upon it. It now belongs to a gentleman of the name of Hamilton" *("Diser. of the Paroch of Bothwell," by Wm. Hamilton, its incumbent, about 1720.)*

MONKLAND HOUSE AND ESTATE are now surrounded by some nice woods, and are prettily situated on the Calder just below the junction with Shotts burn. The house is a very old one, at one time inhabited by monks, as its name indicates, and probably wrested from them at the time of the Reformation. Talking to a man of the district, he said it was one of the "Blue Houses"—which, I suppose, indicates the order of monks who lived in it—old Faskine House being another such. He told me that Monkland and Faskine, and Gartness, too, I was later informed, were at one time united by underground passages. Monkland House is a very quaint looking old place, though much out of repair—however, it is soon about to be inhabited again. The corners are occupied by turrets, and the attic windows appear out of circular projections of the roof. The garden is more or less in ruin, but must have been very fine at one time.

A short distance further up the Calder is the site of old GARTNESS HOUSE, now occupied by a new one, very pleasantly situated. Several cottages form the village of Gartness.

CLELANDS OF MONKLAND.

1st GENERATION.

SIR JAMES CLELAND (194), 1st Cleland of Monkland, was the second son of John Cleland, 3rd Cleland of Faskine, the brother of John, 4th Cleland of Faskine, and great-great-grandson of James Cleland, 7th of that ilk, so that he corresponds with the 14th generation of the Clelands of that ilk

In 1606 he appears as a complainer in the Register of the Privy Council In 1607 the King, "for services to himself and his ancestors performed by James Cleland and his forebears" (this being a mere legal phrase), grants him "the subscribed lands and barony of Monkland," resigned in his favour by D Thomas Hamilton of Binney (*i.e.*, sold to him by Thomas Hamilton). From these lands he received his title of "Monkland"

At Holyrood, 12 Aug , 1607.—" Rex concessit Jacobo Cleland juniori filio legit. quondam Joannis C. de Foscan (inter eum et Agnetem Mureheid ejus sponsam procreato) heredibus ejus et assignatis quibuscunque, irredimabiliter,—terras et baroniam de Monkland subscriptas (viz terras de Pedderisburne et Biownysyde etc., Caldercruikis etc., Airdry etc) quas D. Tho. Hamiltoun de Binny miles, advocatus regius, in favoiem dicti Jac. resignavit, et quas rex,—pio servitio sibi suisque progenitoribus per dictum Jacobum et ejus predecessores prestito, ac pro compositione persoluta, dicto Jacobo de novo dedit, cum libera foresta infra omnes earum bondas, et omnes inseperabiliter ad dictas terras de Brownyside annexint " *(Reg Great Seal)*

In 1611, James Cleland of Monkland was a creditor of Boyd of Badinaith, when the latter died. *(Comm. Rec. Glasgow)*

James Cleland of Monkland was knighted by James I. previous to 1612. He married Mary, daughter of James Stewart of Allantoun, and died about 1633, his son Ludovic succeeding In 1639 " Domine Christina Seaton " is named " relict of the said D Jacobi," and must be his second wife. In 1615, James Cleland of Monkland and George Cleland, his brother-germane, are witnesses to a charter of Ludowic, Duke of Lennox. *(Reg. Great Seal.)* On the 6th September, 1615, this Sir James Cleland of Monkland was, with two others, indicted for trial for treasonably resetting Jesuits, hearing mass, etc , offences very seriously punished in those days of cruelty under the guise of the new religion, but the diet was deserted against them *(MacVeigh's " Scottish Fam History.")* In 1624, Sir James Cleland claims the patronage of the kirks of Monkland and Cadder. The following interesting accounts from the " Register of the Privy Council of Scotland " show the trouble James Cleland managed to give in asserting his rights .—

" Among many cases of disorderly conduct a few may be noted as illustrations of the time. As a specimen of unseemly doings in connection with the Church, the barring of the Kirk of Monkland may be cited. A vacancy having occurred in the ministry of that Kirk, a dispute fell out between two of the heritors, Lord Boyd and Sir James Clelland, as to who should fill it. By a warrant from his Majesty, the Archbishop of Glasgow had presented the Rev. James Fullerton, who had preached with much acceptance to the parishioners. Accordingly the Archbishop had fixed a Sunday when the new minister should be formally presented to the congregation As would appear, Fullerton had been appointed with the approval of Lord Boyd, but not to the content of Sir James Clelland, who now took effective measures to stay further proceedings. On the Saturday night before the appointed Sunday, Clelland, with a large following of his supporters, took posses-

sion of the Kirk, the whole party 'boddin in feare of warre,' and
supplied with ale and tobacco When the next morning the presentee
and the minister who was to admit him appeared at the door of the
Kirk, the garrison forcibly stayed their entrance, and the intended
ceremony was effectually prevented. Such was the story told to the Council by Fullerton and the Archbishop. Circumstantial though it seems,
however, the Council found only one of the non-intrusionists guilty
of a breach of law, and decided that Clelland had been quite within
his right in 'barring of the pursuer's admission in a civil manner'"
(Introduction)

"Complaint of Mr. James Fullerton, Minister at Beath. and James,
Archbishop of Glasgow, for his interest, as follows ·—His Majesty
had presented Mr James Fowllartoun to the sub-deanery of Glasgow,
whereof the Kirk ot Monkland is one of the kirks and had by his
letter to the Archbishop commanded him to proceed with diligence to
his admission, who accordingly appointed the said presentee to preach
at the Kirk of Monkland, on —— last, that the parishioners might
hear him The Archbishop had informed them by letter of the King's
will that Mr James Foullartoun should be placed there, and they
not only showed willingness to hear him but received great content-
ment by his doctrine, whereupon the Archbishop sent Mr Robert
Scot, one of the ministers of Glasgow, with him to the Kirk on ——
last, being Sunday, in order to admit him in terms of his presentation
But Sir James Kneilland of Monkland getting notice thereof and
resolving to oppose the same, he convocated together James Mure-
heid, elder and younger of Lauchop, Robert Hamiltoun of Milne-
burne, James Hammiltoun of Turneley, James Mureheid, bailie of
Hammiltoun, George Anderson of Woodsyde. James Mureheid of
Braidisholme, Alexander Kneilland, brother to the said Sir James,
John Thomsone in Airdreehill, James Pettigrew in Langlone, John
Russill in Broomesyde, George Hill in Caldercruik, Thomas Inglis of
Murdistoun, James Hammiltoun of Broomehill, John Hammiltoun of
Udistoun, James Hammiltoun called the Blacke Laird, William Hammiltoun of Blantyresome, James Mureheid of Shawfilt, William Foir-
syth of Dyke, William Hammiltoun of Wishaw, and George and John
Kneilland, brothers to the said Sir James, 'and with thame he came
to the said Kirk of Monkland upoun the Saturday afoir the Sabbath
foirsaid, all boddin in feare of warre with swords, halberts and stalffes
and uthers weapouns invasive and possest thame selffes of
the said Kirk and remained and abode thairintill drinking aill and
tobacco and committing manie uther abuissis all that night till the
morne.' Then when the said Mr. James Foullertoun and Mr. Robert
Scot came peaceably and craved access to the Kirk, showing their
errand and warrant and his Majesty's presentation and letter they
opposed their entry, 'presented thair weapouns out at the doores unto
thame, threatning thame with present death if they preast to enter the
said Kirk' and so they were forced to retire Charge having been
given to the persons named and Mr James Foullertoun appearing

personally the Archbishop appearing by his procurator Robert Stewart, and all the defenders, except James Hammiltoun of Turneley, the Lords after hearing evidence find that the said George Hill presented 'ane bandit Stalffe' to the said Mr Robert Scot and would not suffer him to enter the kirk to hear the preaching and commit him to ward in the tolbooth of Edinburgh till further order, but they assoilzie the remaining defenders, because the pursuers failed in their proof, 'seeing that it was lawful for the said James to maintain his right and possession of the patronage of the said Kirk by barring of the pursuers admission in a civil manner.' But further the Lords to obtemper his Majesty's desire that the said Kirk be no longer unprovided 'of a minister for teaching of the Word and ministration of the Sacraments to the parochiners of the said Kirk' command the said Archbishop and the minister of the presbytery of Hamilton to see that the said church is served by the said minister *per vires* until it is decided by law to whom the patronage thereof belongs, and they further discharge both the said Mr. James Foullertoun and also Mr. James Johnstoun who was presented to the said Kirk by the same Sir James from preaching or administering the Sacraments therein till then."

Here is engrossed the following letter :—" Charles B Ryght trustie and ryght weilbelovit cousine and counsellour, right trustie and weilbelovit counsellours and ryght trustie and weilbelovit counsellours we greete you weill   In regard the church of Monkland was of a long tyme unprovyded of a preacher becaus of some differences depending in law betwix the Lord Boyd and Sir James Cleilland we wer pleased to write at severall tymes that the same sould be provided, haiving to that effect sent our presentatioun and admissioun to Mr James Foullertoun, preacher at the Church of Baith   But we are since informed that upoun the intendit sattling of the said Mr. James at the said Church of Monkland it was violantlie opposed by the said Sir James, his two brethrein and complices, who (as we ar crediblie informed) in contempt of our pleasure both signified by the said presentation and by our letter written to that effect and shown unto thame, did in armed maner and by convocating our lieges for that effect, barr the said Mr. James his admission, the parochiners from the hearing of the Word and infants frame being baptized, a course not becomming civil men nor good Christianes. Our pleasure thairfoir is that you caus cite the saids persouns before you and after dew tryall of that which is alledged or of suche informationers concerning this purpose as sall be exhibited before you by the said Archbishop if you find thame guiltie that you caus fyne, confyne or otherwayes punishe thame as you sall find the nature of thair offences to have deserved ; and in the mean tyme that you give ordour that the said church be no longer unprovided according to our pleasure heretofore signified to this purpose   So we bid you fairweill. Frome our Court at Theobalder, the 18 of September 1627."

The " Minute Book of Processes " gives the following for the month of November, 1629 .—

Ryott Mr James Foullartoun against Sir James Cleilland.

Holyrood House, 1st April, 1630.

Complaint by Mr. Walter Quhyturde, p c. dean of Glasgow as follows :—He is lawfully provided by his Majesty's presentation under the privy seal to the sub-deanery of Glasgow, and to the Kirks of Calder and Monkland which are united thereto and his said presentation is confirmed by collation and institution from his ordinary and a decree of the Lords of Council and Session He intended by God's grace to sattle him selffe at the Kirk of Monkland which has long been " destitute of ane ordinar pastour " and expected that " now in this happie tyme of peace under his Majesteis blessed government " none would have made violent opposition thereto. Yet Sir James Kneilland of Monkland has resolved by way of " deid, bangstorie and oppressioun ' to hinder this " Quhilk is a point verie unseemelle in this persoun, he being knowin to be ane profest and avowed adversar to the truthe."

He " boasts and minasses, shoares and avowes to debar the compleaner a entrie to the said Kirk, or if he sall preasse to repaire thair unto, to persew him of his lyffe " He and his accomplices lie in wait for this purpose and for a long time past " have watched and guarded the Kirk with convocatioun of his Majesteis Lieges everie Saturday fra night till Sunday after the ordinarie tyme of sermoun," so as to kill the complainer if he should come thither And thus " the exercise of the ministrie and disciplme of the Kirk is altogidder interrupted there and the parochioners cassin louse to follow thair awin humours and appetites " moreover the Said Sir James does what in him lies " to brangle his Majesteis undoubted right of patronage and to intrude himselffe upon his Majesteis right " Parties being called and both compearing and probation being referred to the defender's oath of verity, who denies, the Lords assoilzie him but ordain him to find caution in the books of Privy Council in 5,000 merks for the safety of the pursuer

The following information from the " Munimenta Univ. Glasguensis " deals incidentally with Sir James Cleland's patronage of the kirks of Calder and Monkland, and sets forth the University's claim to that patronage in opposition to Lord Kilmarnock's.

Information of the Caise betwixt my Lord Kilmarnoch and the Universitie of Glasgow (A D 1663)

" The sub-deanerie of Glasgow is a benefice consisting of the Kirks of Calder and Monkland. . The series of the Universities right from the Erle of Haddingtoun, Sir James Cleland, Duke James Hamiltoun, Duke William Hamiltoun, my lady Duchess of Hamiltoun, the Universitie of Glasgow, all quhill wer infeft in the foresaid patronage, and most of ther infeftments ratified in Parliament. . . In 1626 and 1627 Sir James Cleland, one of the Universities authors reduced in foro contradictoris my Lord Kilmarnoch's pretended right "

" Information for the Universitie of Glasgow anent their rights to the sub-deanerie by Sir John Nisbett of Dirleton. . . . Anno 1607, the Earle of Haddingtoune sellis the barronie of Monkland with the annexed right of patronage of the kirkes of Calder and Monkland unto Sir James Cleland, who thairupon is infeft the 12th August, the said yeir . . . Anno 1626 "

" Sir James Cleland presented Mr. James Johnstone to the kirk of Monkland and subdeanerie of Glasgow.   . .

" Anno 1627, there is ane decree obteaned efter long and contentious debait at the instance of Sir James Cleland against Robert Lord Boyd, quhairin the Lord Boyd's right of patronage is reduced, Sir James Cleland's established, and the persone presented by him appointed to be answered conforme to his presentatione . . . Furder the said yeir (i e , 1639) the said Marques of Hamilton buys the forsaid barunie of Monkland with the annexed patronage of the kirks of Calder and Monkland, quhich in effect are the subdeanerie of Glasgow, from Lodovich Cleland eldest son and retoured avi to his father Sir James Cleland .   .   My Lady Duchess of Hamiltoun . . . doeth sell and dispose the said teynds of Monkland and Calder, etc , ...unto the Universitie of Glasgow "

In 1627, James Cleland of Monkland is one of the Custodians of James Cleland of Faskine

In 1630, Sir James is mentioned in a deed to John Hamilton of Airdrie of various lands in Airdiie and Arnbuchill, which lands " omnes olim ad monasterium de Newbottill pertinentes, et de D. Jacobo Cleland de Monkland milite tentas ante generalem dimissionem " *(Reg. Great Seal.)*

In 1634, the lands of Glentores are spoken of as having been held by " D. Jacobo Cleland de Monkland milite ante generalum resignationem " *(Idem.)*

Sir James Cleland of Monkland, Knyt., is named October 29th, 1632. His will was confirmed 21st November, 1633. *(Comm. Hamilton and Campsie.)*

" George Cleland, brother-germane to umqll. Sir James Cleland of Monkland, Knyt.," is mentioned in the will of Christiane Cleland, spous to George Anderson of Woodfyd, April 20, 1635." *(Comm. Rec. Glasg.)*

Christina Cleland, sister of John Cleland, 4th of Foscane, is presumably their aunt.

Sir James Cleland appears in the Commission for the Peace in Lanarkshire in the years 1612, 1614, 1623. *(Reg. Privy Council)*

(b) GEORGE CLELAND (195), brother germane to Sir James, mentioned as above, in 1615, 1627, and 1635. 2nd Cleland of Gartness. Married Margaret Hamilton, daughter of Hamil-

ton of Wishaw, about 1650   Her mother was Beatrix Douglas
of Morton or Gogars. They had a daughter, Anne.

(c) JOHN CLELAND (196), brother germane of Sir James.
Ludovic Cleland of Gartness, Sir James Cleland's son and
heir, is named as his heir, in 1667. *(Inquisitionum ad Gapel-
lam Domini Regis Retornatarum, Lanark.)* Apparently left
no descendants.

(f) ALEXANDER CLELAND (197), brother.   Alexander,
brother germane to Sir James Cleland of Monkland, appears
in 1632, registering a bond. *(Comm. Rec. Glasg.)*

2nd GENERATION.

(a) LUDOVIC CLELAND (198), son and heir of Sir James;
2nd and last Cleland of Monkland, 1st Cleland of Gartness.

Ludovic Cleland, primogenitus D Jacobi militis, graduated M.A. at Glasgow about 1630. *(Munim. Glasg.)*   In
1633 is named as heir of his father, " Domini Jacobi Clealand
de Monkland militis," to the lands of Peddersburne, Broune-
syde, Caldercruikes, Airdrie, etc. *(Idem)* These lands were
afterwards sold in 1639 to James, Marquis of Hamilton, and
with their sale the title of Monkland dropped.

The King, 19th November, 1639, grants to James, Marquis of Hamilton, the lands and barony of Monkland, com-
prehending Peddersburn Broinysye, etc. " Quas Ludovicus
Cleland filius et hæres quondam D. Jacobi Cleland de Monkland militis, cum consensu Domine Christiane Seatoun matris
sua relicte dicti D. Jac., et Georgii C., fratris germani dicti D.
Jac., resignavit." *(Reg. Great Seal.)*

"Ludovic Cleland of Monkland" appears in the testament of John Maxwell, merchant, burgess of Glasgow, 1648.
(Com. Rec. Glasg)

In 1667, Ludovic Cleland, now styled " of Gartness," is
named as heir to John Cleland, his paternal uncle, and
brother germane to Sir James Cleland, and to the lands of
Whytrig, Langbarrelmoss, Darngavell, Hairstanes, Blackrigg,
and " Bluidburne alias Airdriemure," in the parish of Monkland. *(Reg. Great Seal.)*

Apparently Ludovic Cleland of Gartness died without
issue, or transferred Gartness to George Cleland, his uncle,
since in 1672, Anne Cleland, daughter of George Cleland of
Gartness, is served heir to George Cleland. Ludovic Cleland
of Gartness appears, however, as cautioner in 1676. *(Commiss of Glasgow)* Lodovich Cleland and John, his brother,
of Gartness appear again in 1689

(b) JOHN CLELAND (199), brother germane to Ludovic

Cleland of Gartness, died in 1688. Married Bethia Baillie, eldest daughter of Alexander Baillie. In 1692 his widow is married to James Hamilton. In 1701 " the bailies of the burgh of Cannongate and a jury declare that Patrick Hamilton, eldest lawful son of the late Bethia Baillie by her second husband, James Hamilton of Grein, is nearest and lawful heir of provision of the said Bethia's first husband, the late John Cleland," etc. *(Laing Charters)*

(c) MARGARET CLELAND (200), or Main of Lockwood, heir of John Cleland, her brother, and brother to Ludovic Cleland of Gartness, in 1667. Apparently died about this time, without issue, as in 1701 Patrick Hamilton is named John's heir, as above.

(d) ANNE CLELAND (201), daughter of George Cleland, of Gartness, married George Weir of Blackwood They had a son, George Weir, the heir, and a daughter, who died young According to MacVeigh's " Scottish Fam. History," " the Gartness family terminated in an heiress previously to the middle of the 18th century, married to Sir William Vere of Blackwood in the same county." MacVeigh makes the mistake of calling him William Vere, instead of George Vere.   In 1672 she was served heir to George Cleland of Gartness. Her husband was dead in 1681, when her son, George Weir, has as " tutor " (custodian) William Laurie or Weir of Blackwood, his step-grandfather ; in 1694 this son, George Weir, is served heir to his grandfather, George Cleland.   (Note.—William Laurie married the heiress of Blackwood, being her second husband, her first husband being Weir of Blackwood.)

CLELANDS OF GLENHOOFE.

GLENHOOFE HOUSE.—" In the head of this parish (*i e,* New Monkland) upon the water of Luggie, lyeth Glenhoofe ; a pleasant and convenient seat for woods, coall, lyme and barren planting.   It did anciently belong to the Clelands, but now belongs to William Hamilton of Wishaw and James Somervill " *(Wm. Hamilton of Wishaw, in " Descr. of Lanark and Renfrew," 1710)*

1st GENERATION.

GEORGE CLELAND (202), 1st of Glenhoofe, brother of John, 3rd Cleland of Faskine, great-grandson of James, 7th Cleland of that ilk.   Married Margaret Hamilton.   Died before 1577. In 1571 is mentioned as having sided with Queen Mary *(See Faskine branch)*   In 1577 his widow and his second son,

George, have a charter confirmed of the lands of Glenhuiff in the barony of Monkland, signed in 1562.

2nd GENERATION.

GEORGE CLELAND (203), 2nd of Glenhoofe, second son of George, 1st of Glenhoofe. Witness in 1595. *(Reg. Privy Council)* He and his lands of Glenhoofe mentioned in 1603. *(Reg. Great Seal.)*

3rd GENERATION.

(a) GEORGE CLELAND (204), 3rd of Glenhoofe. Mentioned as "younger" in 1595. Mentioned (possibly his father) in 1627, as one of the custodians of James Cleland of Faskine. *(Reg Great Seal.)*

"George Cleland of Glenhoofe, Monkland, 'deceist in the month of Marche, 1647' The inventory of his effects, as follows being ' given upe be John Cleland in Banhaith, sone in law to pe defunct, and exr datine, funogat,' &c Inventare —Item, pe defunct, being ane old aiged man, wtout apr hous or familie, and 1 companie and household with his sone, had no guds or geir, pe tyme of his deceis, except allancylie pe sowme of ffourtie punds Scotts money of yeirlie yaird maill, award to him be Richard Chddisdaill and George Neilsone, weissaris . . . for pe maill of the said twa yairds in Drygait, of pe fol burt of Glasgow ' Conf. July 7, 1655." *(Comm Rec. Glasg. quoted by Hamilton of Wishaw)*

(b) JANET CLELAND (205), his sister. Married — Somerville. Their grandson, James Somerville, is named heir in 1675 to George Cleland, the above *(Inquisitionem, etc.)*

4th GENERATION.

AGNES CLELAND (206), married John Cleland. Daughter of George Cleland of Glenhoof.

AGNES CLELAND, daughter of George Cleland of Glenhuiff, and her husband, JOHN CLELAND, re the Manse of Stobo. Charter of Charles II. in 1649 It formerly belonged to Robert Cleland, merchant burgess of Glasgow : then to JAMES CLELAND, his elder brother ; then to his brother, JOHN CLELAND OF FOSCAN; from him to George Cleland of Glenhuif. *(Munim Univ Glasg.)*

(NOTE.—In the title of the charter, Agnes Cleland is styled " Janet Cleland.")

In The Table, No. 191 —" Charter granted, by Charles II. to Janet and John Cleland, of a tenement and pertinents on the south side of the Drygait of Glasgow, on condition of the said parties paying the sum of ten pounds Scots yearly to the Rector, Principal, Regents, and other members of the Academy and College of Glasgow In this Charter, the King reserves to himself and his successors the right to one chamber and a stable in the back part of the said tenement, and the liberty of walking in the ' gairdene's attached thereto, whenever he or they may visit the Burgh of Glasgow 6 April 1649 ' This document is remarkable as being a Charter under the great seal, bearing to be granted by King Charles II on the 6th April 1649, *in the first year of his reign.* The seal is gone, but the usual doquets of the officers, on the back of the document, bear that it had duly passed the seal." *(Munin. Univ., Glasg)*

This branch apparently ended here, the estates going to a grandnephew of George Cleland, viz., James Somerville.

" James Cleland in Glenhowe," cautioner, 1655. *(Comm. Glasg)* In " ane roole of the Heritors names of Monkland and Calder," in Munim. Univ. Glasg , dated 1659, appears " Glenhuiff, 40s. land. James Cleland, heritor."

" According to local tradition, Cleland of Glenhove was present at Bothwell Brig and never returned, his riderless horse being found grazing in the adjacent woods some days afterwards He took the precaution to secrete his money before setting out, and old natives still point to the hillside in which in their own words ' a bull's hide of gold ' lies hidden. The site of the old ' Castle' of Glenhove is still shown." *(Note by Mr. Harry Cleland, Kilsyth, per P Galbraith, Esq.)*

CLELANDS OF BLAIRLIN.

The origin of this branch of the Clelands is uncertain. " According to local tradition they are descended from the Clelands of Glenhove This is probable enough, as the two places are contiguous." *(Note by Mr. Harry Cleland, Kilsyth.)*

1st GENERATION.

" —— CLELAND (207), descended from the Clelands of that ilk (Monkland Branch). Married Jean Wharrie of the Covenanting Line." Such was the information furnished by my cousins of the furthest back Cleland ancestry, whose descendants could be continuously traced down to the present day, but I have been unable to find the names in the New Monkland registers, unless the following may perhaps apply ·—" 1696, June 14. James Cleland and Janet Qtlair (Whitclair) in fidlersland a lawful son called John " However that may be —— Cleland and Jean Wharrie are given as the parents of James Cleland following, whose descendants are well authenticated." *(Notes by P. Galbraith, Esq.)* JOHN

CLEILAND appears in 1692 in the "Records of the Maltman's Craft," Glasgow.

2nd GENERATION.

JAMES CLELAND (208), of Clayslops, in 1739, afterwards portioner of East Blairlin. Married firstly Annie Linn, and had one child, William Cleland; secondly, Bethia Riddell, and had five sons and two daughters. Died (?) in 1762.

A James Cleland in 1712 rented part of Spreull's Land in the Trongate. This individual probably was an ancestor of James Cleland, LL D , because the latter was related to the Spreull's, and his father, John Cleland, lived in the Trongate. A James Cleland was Baillie of the River and Firth of Clyde in 1730 and 1731.

In the enquiry into the riot on the Malt Tax in June, 1725, in Glasgow, James Cleland is one of those examined by the advocate. "In examining James Cleland, after some other queries, he asked him what he thought of that rabble Mr. Cleland asked him pardon and said, matters were not come to that pass as to be obliged to tell people's thoughts." *(Wodrow's " Analecta." Maitland Club.)*

3rd GENERATION.

Children of James Cleland (208) and Annie Linn.

(1) WILLIAM CLELAND (209). Married 1764 Margaret Riddell, niece of Bethia Riddell 8 children.

Children of James Cleland (208) and Bethia Riddell.

Married 1736.

(2) —— CLELAND (daughter) Born 1739.

(3) MATTHEW CLELAND (210), of Springfield, Cadder Parish, in 1825. Married Marion Naysmith, daughter of Mungo Naysmith, Glasgow. Deacon of the Incorporation of Masons, 1782,-3,-5,-6,-92,-3. 8 children.

(3) GEORGE CLELAND (211). Port Glasgow. Born 1742. Married 1771, Margaret Boyd. Died 1798. 5 children.

(4) JOHN CLELAND (212). Born 1745. Died 1822. Married first Jean Waddell (born 1747, died 1788), secondly, Mary Graham (?) (born 1746, died 1837); by the latter he apparently had no children. Deacon of the Incorporation of Wrights, 1791-2. Was a wright at Grahamstone (in Glasgow). 6 children.

(5) HENRY CLELAND (213). Born 1748.

(6) BETHIA CLELAND (214). Born 1754.

(7) JAMES CLELAND (215). Born 1757. Married, firstly, Margaret Walker; secondly, Margaret King. Wright, Glasgow. Died 1827.

4th GENERATION.

Children of William Cleland (209) and Margaret Riddell.

(1) Ann Cleland. Born 1766. Married Robert Jack, farmer in Rigg, then Muirhead, afterwards Springfield. 8 children.

(2) Bethia Cleland Born 1768. Died young

(3) James Cleland (216). Born 1770. Married, 1794, Agnes Wilson. 9 children.

(4) Thomas Cleland (217). Born 1772.

(5) Bethia Cleland. Born 1774. Married William Moffat. 4 children.

(6) Margaret Cleland. Born 1777. Died, single, about 1860 (?)

(7) William Cleland (218). Born 1779. Married Janet Rodger Mason in Airdrie.

(8) John Cleland (219). Born 1782.

5th GENERATION.

Children of James Cleland (216) and Agnes Wilson.

(1) William Cleland Born 1794. Died young.

(2) Agnes Cleland. Born 1796. Died in infancy.

(3) Agnes Cleland. Born 1797. Died 1877. Married John Darnley, Airdrie. 5 children

(4) Margaret Cleland. Born 1800. Married Andrew Walker. 3 children.

(5) James Cleland (220). Born 1803. Died 1877. Married Marion Cleland, daughter of Matthew Cleland of Springeld and Joanna Moir. No family.

(6) John Cleland (221). Born 1805. Married Jean Balloch

(7) Alexander Cleland. Born 1807. Single. Died 1886.

(8) Thomas Clcland. Born 1809 Single. Died 1892.

(9) Josiah Cleland (222). Born 1812. Married Anne Shaw

Children of William Cleland (218) and Janet Rodger.

Mary (born 1806), William (1808), John (1810), James (1813), Alexander (1815), Matthew (1818), George (1820), Margaret and Christina (1823).

6th GENERATION.

Children of John Cleland (221) and Jean Balloch.

(1) James Cleland (223), in Australia (?).
(2) Mary Cleland. Married James Patterson.
(3) Agnes Cleland. Married — Cameron.

Children of Josiah Cleland (222) and Anne Shaw.

(1) Margaret Cleland. Unmarried.
(2) James Cleland (224). Luggiebank and Kilsyth. Married Janet Esilman.
(3) John Cleland. Died young.
(4) Josiah Cleland (225). Born 1840. Died 1890. Of East Blairlin. Married Annie Buchanan.
(5) Agnes Cleland. Married James Mollison, Glasgow. 10 children.
(6) Robert Cleland. Unmarried
(7) William Cleland. Married. No family.

7th GENERATION.

Children of James Cleland (224) and Janet Esilman

Jessie, James Josiah, Harry Esilman, Jessie, Annie, Alexander Esilman, Annie, Mary, Dora, Margaret Darnley Cleland.

Children of Josiah Cleland (225) and Annie Buchanan.

Janet, Alexander, Josiah and Annie Shaw Buchanan Cleland.

4th GENERATION.

Children of Matthew Cleland (210) and Marion Naysmith.

Janet Cleland, born 1774, married William Dick. Their son, Matthew Dick of Ravenswood, on succeeding to the estate of Springfield, took the name of Cleland. From him the Dick-Clelands are descended.

Bethia Cleland Born 1776. Died young.

James and Matthew died young. John (born 1782), Matthew (231) (1785-1886, married Joanna Muir), George Alexander

Children of George Cleland (211) and Margaret Boyd,

relict of James Lochridge, West Parish, Greenock.
Married 1771.

(1) AGNES CLELAND Married William McFarlane, Port Glasgow. 1 child.
(2) BETHIA CLELAND. Married, first, Farlane McFarlane. Married, second, Daniel O'Flaherty. 2 children.
(3) JOHN CLELAND Born 1775.

(4) JEAN CLELAND. Born 1777. Married Alex. Naismith.
8 children.

(5) JAMES CLELAND (226). Born 1781. Married 1806.
Died 1859.   Collector of Customs, Port Glasgow, latterly
Bristol.   Married Jean Brown, daughter of Richard Brown
and Eleanora Blair, Port Glasgow.   14 children.

Children of John Cleland (212) and Jean Waddell.

(1) JAMES CLELAND (227), LL.D., of Southcroft, was born
in Glasgow, 28th January, 1770, and died on 14th October,
1840, aged 70 years.   In a biographical notice of him by his
grandson, James Cleland Burns, in 1877, it is stated that his
forefathers lived in New Monkland; and a footnote infers that
they were descended from the Clelands of Monkland

In 1800 he became a member of the Town Council; in
1806 a Bailie of Glasgow, in 1812, Treasurer to the City;
and from 1814 to 1834 Superintendent of Public Works.   On
his retirement, in 1834, " the leading merchants resolved that
a subscription should be immediately instituted with the view
of presenting him with some tangible mark of the esteem in
which his ' unwearied and gratuitous statistical labours' were
held by the community."   A sum of £4,600 was raised, " which
the Committee resolved should be expended on the erection of
a productive building in a suitable part of the town, and to be
designated ' The Cleland Testimonial.'   The site chosen was
in Buchanan Street, and the pile, which is ornate and sub-
stantial, was, on its completion, given over to the distinguished
statist, to be handed down as an honoured heirloom in his
family."   The building may still be seen, with its name inscribed above it, at the corner of Buchanan Street, Glasgow.
It has recently been sold, and the proceeds distributed
amongst the descendants of James Cleland.   " Dr. Cleland
was the first to construct statistical tables, by which
reliable data is afforded of determining the probable average
duration of life, both in towns and counties."   As an analyst
and statistician he published many works (a list of which
appears at the end of this work under "Bibliotheca Cle-
landica "), indicating great trouble and care in their compilation and endless research.

" Cleland Gold Medal.—Dr James Cleland, Superintendent of Public Works in Glasgow, who died 14th October,
1840, founded a Gold Medal of the value of Ten Guineas, to be
bestowed in alternate years on a student of Divinity and a
student of Natural Philosophy, as a prize for the best essay on

any subject to be prescribed by the Principal and Professors of the University." *(University Calendar.)*

He married, firstly, Margaret Rodger, in 1792, secondly, Mary Stewart, in 1811, and had issue by both marriages.

(2) AGNES CLELAND. Born 1763, died 1827. Married John Buchanan, manufacturer, Glasgow. The Comrie Thomsons are descended from her.

Children of James Cleland (215) and Margaret Walker.

(1) Helen Cleland. Born 1800
(2) Henry Cleland (228)   Born 1802.

Children of the above James Cleland (215) and Margaret King.

(1) Margaret Rodger Cleland   Born 1807.   Married Walter McKinlay. Went to Australia. No family.
(2) George Cleland (229), M.D   Born 1809. Abbotsford Place, Glasgow. Married Sophia Lang   Died 1844.
(3) James Cleland. Born 1811.
(4) Jean Cleland. Born 1812. Died 1815
(5) John Cleland. Born 1815.
(6) Charles Cleland (230). Born 1817. Married Jane McKendrick. Died 1884.
(7) Helen King Cleland. Born 1821   Married Charles Wilson, Architect, Glasgow. 6 children.

5th GENERATION.

Children of Matthew Cleland (231) and Joanna Muir.

(1) Barbara Cleland   Born 1806. Married.
(2) Marion Cleland.   Married James Cleland of East Blairlin. Born 1812. Died 1877.
(3) John Cleland. Born 1825. Died (single) 1867.

Children of James Cleland (226) and Jean Brown

George (1807, died young), Richard (1809-1891, Captain on Cunard Line, married Anne Christie, 3 children), James (1810-1893, single), Eleanora (1812-1852, married Lieutenant, afterwards Major-General, Alex. Woodburn, C.B), Archibald Boyle, Alex. Brown (M.D., married Fanny Roberts, 2 children), Margaret, Donald Brown (1819-1834), William Hamilton, Jean, Bethia, Jean, Robert Gilkison, Elizabeth Ann (married George Henry Hussey).

Eleanora Cleland and Alexander Woodburn had offspring —Archibald Woodburn, Jane Cleland Woodburn (married Sir F. W. Beattie, M.D., Gowran Castle, Co. Kilkenny), Archibald,

James, Eleanora Margaret, Anne Isabella (married J F. Norris, Q.C), Susanna Blair, Alexandrina Elizabeth.

Children of James Cleland (227) and Margaret Rodger.

(1) JANE CLELAND.—Born 1793, died 1877. Married in 1822 George Burns, afterwards Sir George Burns, Bart., of the Cunard Shipping Line. Their children were John Burns, afterwards 1st Lord Inverclyde; James Cleland Burns; and a Miss Burns, who married Charles Reddie.

(2) JOHN CLELAND.—Born 1794, died about 1848. Writer, Glasgow. Married Catherine Reid, a poetess and musician, daughter of William Reid, poet of Glasgow. Their only surviving daughter, Elizabeth Cleland (born 1829, died 1871) married John Hamilton, B.D., a master engineer and inventor of the governor for marine engines, etc.

(3) WILLIAM CLELAND.—Went to Australia. His son, William Cleland, paid a visit to the Old Country many years ago.

(4) MARGARET CLELAND, married Dr. Charles Ritchie. Several children.

Children of the above James Cleland (227) and Mary Stewart.

(5) ALEXANDER STEWART CLELAND.—Born 1812, married Martha Brown in 1835. Two sons, who died young, and three daughters—Mary Stewart, married Andrew Philp; Catherine Alice, married Napier Gordon Glassford, born 1845; and Christina, born 1847.

(6) HENRY WILSON CLELAND, M.D —Died about 1844. No descendants.

(7) JAMES DENNISTON CLELAND —Married a Spanish lady at Buenos Ayres. Son killed when a child, daughter, Rosa Corinna, married.

Children of Dr. George Cleland (229) and Sophia Lang.

(1) Sophia Lang Cleland, Ealing.
(2) Margaret Cleland, Ealing.

Children of Charles Cleland (230) and Jane McKendrick.

(1) Charles J. Cleland —Born 1867; married, in 1888, Janet Houston Burrell. Bailie of Glasgow. Three children. (1) Isabella Guthrie Cleland (born 1889), (2) Jean Cleland (born 1890), (3) Jessie Muriel Cleland (born 1893).

(2) James William Cleland.—Born 1874. Barrister and Member of London County Council.

CLELANDS OF UNDER-THE-BANK, STONYPATH, AND BARBADOES.

1st GENERATION.

1593. JAMES CLELAND, UNDER-THE-BANK, died November.

2nd GENERATION.

1586. JAMES KNELAND, YOUNGER, of Nether-bank, mentioned. *(Reg. Great Seal.)* This must be a son of the first-mentioned.

WILLIAM KNELAND, son of the first-named, was murdered by Adam Weir, in Auchtragyminill, Lesmahago, in 1593. *(Reg. Privy Seal.)*

1612-1632 GAVIN CLELAND, brother and heir of the late James Cleland of Under-bank, mentioned; in 1618 a commission is given to him to apprehend various persons for murder; he appears again in 1628. *(Reg Great Seal and Privy Council.)* He made his will in 1629, and died in 1632. The will was confirmed in 1635, Robert Lockhart, Park of Nemphlar, Lanark, his father-in-law, being appointed tutor to his bairns, James and Jean Cleland. *(Lanark Comm. Rec.)*

3rd GENERATION.

JAMES CLELAND OF STONYPATH.—"Had at least two sons *(Lyon Register)*, the elder might perhaps be a Gavin, in accordance with a prevalent custom well known, whilst the other was Professor William Cleland." *(Notes by J.B.D., in "Hamilton Advertiser," 1890)*

JEAN CLELAND, his sister.

4th GENERATION.

GAVIN CLELAND.—Probably the pupil of the 4th Class, Glasgow College, 1682

"WILLIAM CLELAND, professor of physick in the island of Barbadoes, in America, second lawful son to James Cleland of Stonypath, in the County of Tweed-dale, which James was lawful son to Gavin Cleland of Underbank in the County of Clydesdale, which family is descended from the ancient family of the Clelands of that ilk, in the same county," records his arms in the Lyon Register, November 26th, 1692. They are:—"Azure, a hare salient argent, with a hunting horn about his neck, vert, garnished, and stringed or, within a bordure wavy of the second, charged with three crescents and as many roses; interchanged gules; crest, a rose, gules, barbed and stalked vert; motto, Fragrat, delectat et sanat."

This William Cleland is the Colonel William Cleland described by Swift in his "Journal to Stella," as intriguing in 1712-13 for the Governorship of Barbadoes, and whom he describes as a "true Scotchman." The passage is quoted under the name of Major William Cleland, 17th of that ilk, with whom this individual had been confounded by Scott.

A writer in "Notes and Queries," 1866, says of him that "he really was the son of JAMES CLELAND OF STONEPATH, Peebles (see his will, August 24th, 1718, proved in London); and, as it appears, got the Barbadoes appointment, and died in a very few years. The heraldries give the arms of Clelland of Barbadoes differenced from those of the head of the family"

CLELANDS OF LITTLE HARESHAW (IN SHOTTS.)

The Clelands of Little Hareshaw were an older branch than Auchenlee. I find William Cleland in the Sessions Records from 1650 till 1680. He was a Commissioner of Supply in 1664, and in 1685-90, a Commissioner for Militia in 1689, and in 1704, William Cleland, jun , is a Commissioner of Supply. In 1726 I find him and William Cleland of Auchenlee making proposals to buy the lands of Meikle Hareshaw from James Inglis. *(Grossart, Thomson's Acts of Scotch Parliament)*

William Cleland in Little Hauschaw appears in 1649 *(Comm Glasgow)* He appears again in 1661

"Anna Hamiltone, relict of the deceased William Cleland of Hairschaw in the parish of Shotts and Sheriffdome of Lanark, William Cleland of Hairschaw, our eldest sone, subscryvat att Little Hairshaw, 7th May, 1729 Before these Witnesses Andrew, Alexander and John Clelands my sons." *(Comm. Glasgow)*

CLELANDS IN CROSSFORD BOAT.

1494. PATRICK CLELAND of Crossford Boat. On 22nd October, 1494, Stevin Lokart obtained a decree from the "Lords of Council" against Patric Cleland and Richard Hasty for the profits of the ferry-boat at the Crossford of Water of Clyde for the 15 years preceding. *(J B.D., in "Hamilton Advertiser," 1890)*

1593, 1594. WILLIAM CLELAND, brother of Cleland in Corsfurde.

"Complaint by John M'Kgill, advocate, Sir David Lindsay of the Mount, Lyon King of Arms and others, as follows, that when a messenger was sent with the spouse of John M'Kgill and servants to uplift certain duties belonging to him in Lesmahago, at Bankheid William Cleland brother of Cleland in Corsfurde (many others mentioned with him) all armed, wounded said messenger, forcibly broke open doors, seized the servants, took them captive and detained them in a 'mure' without meat or drink for 24 hours—the foresaid principal offenders are all denounced as defaulters " *(Reg Privy Council)*

1665. JAMES CLELAND, in Crossford-boat, test. conf

1682 JOHN CLELAND in Crossford Boat, fugitived in the Covenanting troubles A test-burner in 1682

1695. JAMES CLELAND, smith, in Crossford Boat, Lesmahago Parish.

1702 DANIEL, son to James Cleland in Crossford Boat. *(Reg. Lesmahago.)*

CLELANDS IN CAMBUSNETHAN.

1589-1591. ALEXANDER CLELAND, son of John Cleland in Cambusnethan. William Somerville of Spitteltoun cautioned not to harm Alexander. *(Reg. Privy Council.)*

1630. JOHN CLELAND, younger, in the toun of Cambusnethan, enters into a bond. *(Comm. Glasg)*

1638 ALEX. CLELAND in Eivertoun of Cambusnethan. *(Comm Glasg.)*

1656. " JOHN CLELAND, elder, in the Overtoun of Cambusnathan, in name and behalf of JAMES, JONET, and MARIOUN CLELANDS his childreing." *(Comm. Glasg.)*

CLELANDS OF ABBEY GREVE, LANARKSHIRE.

1704-1724 JAMES CLELAND and Agnes (?) Allan appear several times in the Lesmahago Register, baptising JAMES and WILLIAM, etc., about 1704, and a Robert in 1711. He is mentioned in 1724 as a writer in drawing up the will of Andrew Leiper of Abbeygrieve.

1748. JAMES CLELAND in Clyde Bridgend of Lanark, mentioned as one of those called to give evidence in regard to some rebels of the " 45 " (Is he James Cleland of Abbeygrieve, or James Cleland of Crossford?)

CLELANDS OF DEVON.

1660. THOMAS CLELAND, minister of the Gospel at Chivelston in Devon, is author in 1660 of a pamphlet, "The Christian's Encouragement to Believe; or a sermon preached on Rom. x. xi."

—— CLELAND. Admiral An old friend of John Cleland, F.R.S , informed him many years ago that he had seen the gravestone of such a person in a West of England cemetery.

A writer in " Notes and Queries " in 1866 says the Clelands of Konnoblehill made Cleland " Cleuland," and so Cleveland, by which last appellation their representatives, now of Tapley, Devonshire, are known. He gives no authority for this statement.

CLELANDS WHOSE GENEALOGICAL POSITION IS UNKNOWN.

1501. "NICHOLAIO KNELANDIS t. Lundoris landis, with ane memoriall concerning the same." *(Exchequer Rolls. Vol. XI., p 91)*

1539 JOHN KNELAND, tenant IN DRUMMABEN. *(Exchequer Rolls.)*

1544. "ADAMO KNELAND," witness to a charter of " Domine Isobelle Hume." *(Reg Great Seal)*

1546 " MARIOTA CLELAND," wife of Alexander Lockart of Cleghorn, mentioned in a deed. *(Reg. Great Seal.)* Life-rent reserved to her in 1568, 1580. *(Thomson's Acts)*

1550 JOHN KNELAND, tenant in LANGNEWTON. *(Reg. Great Seal.)*

1578, 1584, 1605. JAMES CLELAND, "servus D. Jacobi Hamilton de Crawfuird Johne " (1578).

John Logan of Coustoun appears before the King, etc , and renounces a gift of the escheat goods of George Douglas, son of George Douglas of Parkheid, now a rebel, the renunciation being in favour of *James Cleland*, servitor to the Earl of Arran, to the effect that the King's gift to the said James and his heirs may be " past and exped." *(Reg. Privy Council, 1584.)*

Servus Duke of Lennox (1605). *(Reg Great Seal.)*

1580, 1581 JOHN CLELAND to attend the wapenschaw with his " bandit staff." *(Records of Burgh of Lanark.)*

1583. WILLIAM CLELAND, maltman (mentioned again 1586), his son JOHN CLELAND and ALEXANDER CLELAND, dwelling IN GLASGOW, probably a near relative, mentioned in a deed in Glasgow protocols.

1588. ISABELLA CLELAND, wife of James Bell, merchant. *(Glasgow Protocols.)* In 1630 she appears as relict of James Bell. *(Sheriff's Court Books, Glasgow.)*

1604. ALEX CLELAND, "servus" of the Duke of Lennox (1604). Living in Wester Lechie (1606). *(Reg. Great Seal.)*

1605. John Cleland, "servus" Lord Torpichen.

1609. James Cleland in Kirknewton Various persons bound over not to hurt him and others *(Reg. Privy Council)*

1609. Elias Kneland, in the Orkneys.

Elias Kneland, in the Earl of Orkney's service, with others, instigated by the Earl of Orkney, came to complainer's, Thomas Blak, his Majesty's servitor, dwelling house, in the Isle of Quhinslay in Zetland, violently broke up the doors, entered with drawn swords in their hands, sought complainer everywhere, and "sua effrayit his spouse that she then parted with bairn," etc. *(Reg. Privy Council.)*

Elias Kneland, in Orkney, and others deride the King's proclamation and attack various people. 1611. *(p 163.)*

1613 John Kneland of Thornehill.—On 15th January, 1613, James Carmichell and John Kneland, dwelling in Thornehill, are denounced rebels for not appearing to answer a charge for the "odious and detestable murder of the said late Johnne Weir," and authority is given to convene the leiges for their apprehension. *(Reg. Privy Council.)*

1615. John Kneland of Tannochie.—Sale of land to him. *(Reg. Great Seal.)*

1617 William Kneiland in Strabok mentioned. *(Reg Great Seal.)*

1617. John Kneland, son of Robert Kneland in Farne-law.

Johnne Kneland, son of Robert Kneland in Farnelaw, and John Kirkpatrick lie in irons in the Tolbooth of Edinburgh for 14 weeks for the alledged murder of Andrew Kyninmouth. His Majesty being informed of their innocence is asked to grant them a remission Helen Litle, John Cleland's spouse is mentioned, 1617. *(Reg. Privy Council)*

1617. M. Cleland, Durisdeir, signs in 1617 a document in reference to uniting Torren's Kirk with Kilbryde Kirk, and disposing the same to the College of Glasgow. *(Munim. Univ. Glasg.)*

1617. Angus Cleland, cordiner in Edinburgh, signs a petition on behalf of his trade (1617).

John Cleland, cordiner, Edinburgh, mentioned in 1607. Mentioned again in 1620.

"Two Bailies of the Burgh of the Cannogait and Thomas Lowrie burgess thus make complaint against the town of Edinburgh in the matter of the freedom of the Edinburgh Market to purchasers from the Cannogait. The bailies of Edinburgh and Mungo Bankis their officer apprehended Lowrie and committed him to the tolbooth and will not release him till he pay 20/ as unlaw for having 'coft certane hydis for his work, publichtlie in mercat tyme of day ' Although

'Lyke oppressioun' has often been attempted before against the crafts
of the Cannogait this last act has proceeded anly from the 'greed and
instigation' of *Johnne Kneland* deacon of the cordiners of Edinburgh
and others who desire to keep for themselves the whole profit of the
said public market   Charge given to *Kneland* and others to answer
and the bailies and said *Cleland* and others being present a defence is
produced   The Lords decern against the defenders and ordain Lowrie
to be set at liberty"

"Complaint by bailies of burgh of Cannogait against the cordiners
of Edinburgh for denying them the freedom of the market. The same
Lowrie and others complain that *Johnne Kneland*, deacon of the
cordiners of Edinburgh and other cordiners 'be way of bagastrie' reft
from complaines ten pairs of shoes which they still detain"

"2nd March 1607 while complainers were selling their goods in the
market Johne Kneland and others 'violantlie and perforce overwhelmed
and dang doun the saidis complenaris standis and tred thair schone
and mullis in the Myrris and gutteris' Charge is given to *Kneland*
and the others to answer and all being present the Lords ordain the
defenders to restore the said goods to pursuers and to keep good neighbourhood with them in time coming." *(Reg Privy Council.)*

1618. "M. JOSEPHO CLELAND, servitor Episcopi Candide-
case." Witness *(Reg. Great Seal)*

1618. ROGER CLELAND IN RAVINSHEUCH, cited for contra-
vening the acts against "carrying arms and slaughtering wild
foll and dier " *(Reg Privy Coun.)*

1620, 1625 PATTRICK KNELANDS, skinner, in Potterow
(1620). JOHN and PATRICK KNEILAND charged with assault at
the "Societie port of Edinburgh." (1625.) *(Reg. Privy
Council.)*

1621 JOHN CLELAND, messenger. *(Reg. Privy Council.)*

1622. WILLIAM CLELAND IN KUSHOBLE, principal, and ALEX-
ANDER CLELAND IN SCHAWES, cautioner, in borrowing a sum of
money. *(Comm. Rec. Glasgow.)*   In 1629, this Alexander
Cleland of Shawes, son of umq^ee JAMES CLELAND IN SHAWS,
enters into a bond in which his "rowme and mailing of
Schaws" is mentioned *(Sheriff Court Books, Glasgow)*

WILLIAM CLELAND IN SHAWIS, tutor to WILLIAM and
JAMES, sons of JAMES CLELAND IN CLELINGTON, his brother germane (1670). (? By a writer in "Hamilton Advertiser," is
this younger William Cleland the Cameronian Colonel?)
WILLIAM CLELAND, SOUTH SHAWS, 1734, assessed at £80.

1623. WILLIAM KNEILAND IN PRESTON. *(Reg. Great Seal.)*

1623. MARION CLELAND, Halhill, test. conf.

1624. EUPHAMIE CLELAND, relict of umqll. Malcom Fleming. *(Sheriff's Books, Glasgow.)*

1624. MRS JAMES CLELAND, AUCHNOTOROCH, test. conf

1625 Mrs Arthur Cleland, Brydokhill (Brodie Hill), test. conf.

1629. Jean Cleilland in Corehouse Mills and others to be apprehended for.

"Commission under the signet of Mr. John Hamiltoun of Bayanie, etc , to search for, apprehend and examine . . . [16 names] .

. . and Jean Cleilland in Corehouse Mills who 'as commoem practisers of the detestable crymes of Witchecraft, using of charmes and enchantments, laying on and taking aff of sicknesses and uthers devilish practises' as the depositions of Isobel Gray, lately 'bruit for Witchecraft both before her convictions and at her death' show." *(Reg Privy Council.)*

1630. A bond is registered in which the parties agree to pay "Andro Cleland" lawfull son to Alexander Cleland elder in Cultness the sume of ane hundrethe merks In 1650 John Cleland in Cultness acknowledges a debt. In 1661 occur John Cleland in Cultness and James Cleland, "collheware," in Cultness. *(Comm Glasg)*

1631. James Cleland in Nudrie mentioned. *(Reg. Privy Council.)*

1632 Mr. George Cleland, minister of Durisdeir, contributes "20 lib" to the Glasgow College Library in 1632. Test. confirmed by his spouse, Jean Wilson, in 1657.

1633. Alexander Cleland and John Cleland, sons to Alexander Cleland, appear as witnesses to a bond of Margaret Setoun, Lady Kilcrewch *(Comm. Rec Glasg.)*

1636 Archibald Cleland, servitor to Sir Archibald Stewart, witness *(Com. Rec Glasg.)*

1644. James Cleland in Ridleland borrows 20 merks. *(Comm Rec. Glasg.)*

1646. William Cleland and William Cleland, Jun., with others, had to do penance before the congregation for "their complyance with the enemy," having, when Montrose, after Kilsyth, halted near the west-end of the Parish of Shotts on his journey southwards. either joined his forces or procured a protection from him *(Vide Grossart)*

1647. William Cleland, servitor to James Stark, witness. *(Comm Rec. Glasg.)*

1648. "Wilihame Cleland of Knowbil," signs a bond. *(Com. Rec Glasg.)*

1648. William Cleland in Wardheid, witness; William Cleland in Ubirdheid signs a bond in 1649 (probably the same): Margrett Cleland, daughter to umqll. Hew Cleland in Warl'. id. 1648. *(Com Rec Glasg.)*

1649 ALEXANDER CLELAND IN WHYTFOORD. *(Comm. Glasg)*

1651. THOMAS CLELAND, JAMES CLELLAND, elders and deacons of the kirk. *(Kirk-Session Records of Lesmahago.)*

1652 JOHN CLELAND, indweller in Clendighill, lends 100 merks. *(Com Rec. Glasgow)*

1655. "WILLIAM CLELAND and Margaret Stirling, spouses, in Warlheid, and JAMES CLELAND, our lawfull sone." *(Comm. Glasg.)*

1656, 1711. JAMES CLELAND IN BATE · JAMES CLELAND IN HALFLECT, in list of elders. Clelands of Halflect appear in Lesmahago Register about 1711.

1659 "Gayne Dykheid and Cleddans, Merkland, WILLIAM CLELAND, heritor " *(Munim. Univ. Glasg.)*

1661. JOHN CLELLAND IN WHYTCRAIGHEID. *(Comm. Glasg.)*

1661. ROBERT CLELAND IN JERVESTOUN *(Comm Glasg.)*

1662. WILLIAM CLELAND IN SHEALAND fined £240. *(Thomson.)* This was one of the fines imposed by Middleton, in Parliament 1662, on those excepted from the Act of Indemnity. *(Wodrow.)*

1663. JOHN CLELAND, minister, of Stow, confined to his parish *(Wodrow.)*

1668. JAMES CLELAND in Overtoun of Dalserf. Test conf.

Parish of Dalziel.

1658 August 1st, baptized ———, son to John Cleland, in the Parish of Camnethan.

October 9th, John, son to Walter Cleland, in the Parish of Camnethan.

1661. October 20th, baptized James, son to James Cleland, in the Parish of Bothwell.

1662 February 16th, baptized Margaret, daughter to Walter Cleland, in the Parish of Camnethan

Parish of Lanark.

1656 Thomas, lawful son to John Cleland, born 20th March, baptized 28th.

1658 (?) Andrew, lawful son to John Cleland, born 10th May, baptized 16th. Witnesses, David Park and George Gray.

Parish of Hamilton.

1658. James Cleland had a child born called James.

Parish of Camnethan.

1658 William Cleland has a child baptized called Thomas. 2nd May.

1658. William Cleland has a child baptized called Joan. 19th June.

1659. James Cleland has a child baptized called Alexander. 10th April.

1659. Alexander Cleland has a child born, Margaret.

1659. James Cleland has a child baptized called Andrew. 24th April, 1659.

1660. William Cleland has a child baptized called Janet. March.

1660. James Cleland, collr., has a child baptized called Barbara. 19th April.

1660. William Cleland has a child baptized called Alexander 22nd July.

1660. Johne Cleland has a child baptized called Agnes. 9th September.

1664 William Cleland has a child baptized called Johne. 3rd January

1664 " Be it kend to all men be thir present letters me EDWARD CLELAND now indweller in the CANONGAIT, For the speciall love and faver quhilh I have and beir to JAMES CLELAND my eldest lawful sone, and for dyvers uther causes, etc. Constitute and ordaine the said James Cleland, my very lawfull, etc., assignay In and to the principal debts, etc., efter specifict —100 merks principall adebitted to me be James Cleland of Foscane," etc. *(Comm Glasg)*

1664-168—. DAVID, son to ANDREW CLELAND IN HOWMAIN'S, fugitived in Covenanting troubles. The test. of Andrew Cleland's spouse was confirmed in 1664.

1665. "JAMES CLELAND IN VAIRDHEID borrowit fra Elspeth Cleland, his sister, 100 merks." *(Comm. Glasg.)*

1666 ELIZABETH CLELAND, relict of umql. John French, burgess of Glasgow. *(Comm. Rec.)*

1673. JOHN CLEILLAND escapes from the prison at Lanark *(Lanark Records)*

1684 Proclamation, with list of fugitives, ordering their apprehension and forbidding any to harbour or comfort the said persons. Amongst many names appear *(Wodrow)* :—

Bothwell Parish.—ARTHUR CLELAND in Westfield in Lauchop's Land.

Douglas.—WILLIAM CLELAND, son to Thomas Cleland in Douglas. THOMAS CLELAND for reset of his son.
Lesmahago.—DAVID CLELAND, son to Andrew Cleland in Howmains. JOHN CLELAND in Crossford Boat.
Carluke.—JOHN CLELAND, portioner, of Yuilshiels.
Cambusnethan.—ANDREW CLELAND in Fimerton.

1688-1698. GEORGE CLELLAND was ordained at Rosehall, on the 1st October, 1688, and all that is known of him is that he was a probationer residing within the bounds of the Presbytery of Edinburgh. On the 26th April, 1698, an elder from Shotts reports to the Presbytery of Hamilton, that Mr Cleland, minister, is sick, and desires a supply of preaching. He died the same year. *(Grossart.)*

1689, 1695 JAMES CLELAND OF PITENNES, overseer for the election of magistrates for Montrose (1689); Commissioner of Supply for Fife (1695). *(Thomson)*

1689-1702. CLELAND, ROBERT. A prominent man at the coming of the Prince of Orange. Commissioner to Parliament for Anstruther Wester (1689-1700); signs the Act declaring the legality of the meeting of estates summoned by the Prince of Orange, 1689; signs a letter of congratulation to King William, 1689; the Association in his defence, 1696; Commissioner on the claims of persons restored from forfeiture, 1690; on committee for disputed elections, 1696; votes for an Act concerning Caledonia, 1701; dissents from continuing the forces till December, 1702 *(Thomson's Acts)* Probably the Writer, Edinburgh, whose arms are registered as " az a hare salient and guardant arg. with a hunting horn about his neck vert garnished gu. within a bordure counter-company of the second and first." Probably also the Robert Cleland of Hillhouse, Commissioner of Supply for Fife, 1704.

1689 SAMUEL CLEILLAND in Capt. Stevenson's Roll of Cameronian Regiment.

JAMES CLEILLAND in Capt. Stevenson's Roll of Cameronian Regiment.

JOHN CLELAND in Col. Cleland's Roll

1695. In Lesmahago Poll-tax Records :—

JANET CLELAND, mother of Gavin Fairservice.

JANET CLELLAND, spouse of James Hamilton in Threepwood.

MARY CLELLAND, spouse to William Jack.

JEAN CLELLAND, daughter of Janet Jack.

JANET CLELLAND, spouse of James Smith in Holmhead.

1680. JANET CLELAND visited Hackston in the vault, and

humanely brought a surgeon to him. (She may have been John Haddow's wife.) *(Wodrow.)*

1682. AGNES CLEILAND in Douglas, mentioned. (May have been Haddow's wife, or, as is more probable, the wife of George Weir of Blackwood)

ARTHUR CLELAND in Auchnottroch; Marion Young, his spouse. JOHN CLELAND, his son. JAMES CLELAND, his son.

MARIE CLELLAND, daughter to Arthur.

AGNES CLELLAND, wife of William Weir in Garrellwood.

JEAN CLELLAND in Garrelwood.

ELIZABETH CLELAND, wife of James Lean in Boreland

WILLIAM CLELAND in Bighead.

MARGARET CLELLAND, wife to John Steven in Auchleck.

1696. Four Edinburgh Clelands:—JAMES, a merchant, JAMES, junior (his son); ALEXANDER, junior, merchant; and JOHN (evidently a brother of Alexander) had shares in the Darien Expedition

1695, 1696. JAMES CLELAND, maltman, indweller in Douglas, married Elizabeth Pirie. Witness in 1695 and 1696. His son, JAMES, baptized 1695. His son, DAVID, baptized 1696 His daughter, ANNA, baptized 1697.

1703. JAMES CLELAND, for mending a poor child's arm, £2. *(Annals of Lesmahago.)*

1704 WILLIAM CLELAND, session-clerk in Crawford John, has kept his books "exceedingly ill-spelled and ill-worded, whereby it is unintelligible and nonsense in many places." *(Presby. Reg Lanark.)*

1703. RODGER CLELLAND, appointed by the baillies, etc., of *Lanark* to report on the meal market.

1709-1711. JOHN CLELAND, merchant, Dean of Guild, *Lanark.* Frequently mentioned in the Records.

1713. JOHN CLYLAND at a general meeting of the "witnessing remnants of the Presbyterians in Scotland," at Crawfordjohn.

1735. MARGARET CLELAND, daughter and heir of JAMES CLELAND, senior merchant in Glasgow. Sasine *(Glasgow Protocols.)* Spouse to John Clatchie, Jun., manufacturer.

1770. WILLIAM CLELAND, an operative weaver, assistant pastor to the Old Scot's Independents, Albion Street Chapel, Glasgow, between 1770-1807 *(Cleland's Enumer. of Inhabitants of Glasg)*

1774 JAMES CLELAND IN COMENHILL died, aged 77. *(Lesmahago Churchyard.)*

1788 ARTHUR CLELAND died, aged 73 years. *(Lesmahago Churchyard.)*

1813. Margaret Stark, spouse to ARTHUR CLELAND IN BLACKHILL, died, aged 75 years. *(Lesmahago Churchyard.)*

—— CLELAND, an Army surgeon, is mentioned in Wylde's "Aural Surgery," one of the earliest books on that subject, as having been the first to practice catheterization of the Eustachian tube.

1820. "About 1820 there were great disturbances about the Reform Bills, and a man Richmond took advantage of the discontent of the lower classes to stir up a rebellion so that he might make money by giving evidence against them. In April, about thirty weavers armed themselves and started off from Glasgow to take Stirling. They were met at Bonnymuir by a troop of Hussars and taken prisoners. Some were hanged and the majority were transported to Sydney, among them being a JAMES CLELAND, smith, of Glasgow. Mackenzie afterwards exposed the plot of this man Richmond, and on the 21st of July, 1835, William IV. granted a free pardon to these men. This pardon actually took three years to reach these men, some of whom had settled in Sydney." *(Condensed from Mackenzie's Reminiscences of Glasgow.)*

1831. JOHN CLELAND, schoolmaster, Old or West Monkland. *(Cleland's Enum.)*

CLELANDS WHO WERE STUDENTS AT THE UNIVERSITIES OF GLASGOW AND EDINBURGH.

GLASGOW.

From "Munimenta Universitatis Glasguensis" and Addison's Roll of Graduates (1727-1897).

1675. ALEXANDER CLELAND—Pupil of the '4th Class' (Possibly the son of James Cleland, second son of James Cleland, 13th of that ilk.)

1657. ARCHIBALD CLELAND—Pupil of the '4th Class' (Possibly Archibald Cleland of Connoblehill, mentioned in 1710.)

1598 CLAUD CLELAND—Takes the oath. (Probably Claud Cleland, son of William Cleland, 12th of that ilk, mentioned in 1603.)

1682. GAVIN CLELAND—Pupil of the '4th Class.' (Probably son of James Cleland of Stonypath and brother of Prof. Wm. Cleland of Barbadoes.)

1699. JAMES CLELAND—D. Cleland de eodem haeres. Pupil of the '4th Class' (Who is this James Cleland? If his age at entering the College was about 13, a usual age, he cannot have been the son of William Cleland, the Commissioner of Customs, who was born in 1674, and could only be 25 at this time. He must have been the son of the Alexander Cleland, self-styled of that ilk, who about 1680 married a daughter of Hamilton of Wishaw)

1630. JAMES CLELAND AND JOHN CLELAND—' Ascripti Novitii Sequentes.' (Are these possibly the sons of Alexander Cleland, 14th of that ilk ? His second or third son is said to have been a John. If they are they cannot have been more than 10 years old It is noteworthy that in 1632 this Alexander subscribes to the Library Fund)

1642, 1644. In 1642, JAMES CLELAND is mentioned. In 1644, James Cleland laureated, evidently the same person in both instances.

1663 JAMES CLELAND—Pupil of the ' 4th Class '

1671. JAMES CLELAND—Pupil of the ' 4th Class.'

1619-1623 JOHN CLELAND—' Adscriptus,' 1619; laureated, 1622; mentioned 1623. (Possibly the brother of Alexander Cleland, 14th of that ilk, mentioned in 1632)

1630 JOHN CLELAND—Mentioned above with James

1725, 1726 JOHN CLELAND—Laureated (with Thomas Cleland), 1725; theological student, 1726

1613-1636 JOSEPH CLELAND—His name inscribed, 1610, laureated, 1613; subscribes two dollars for the Library, 1636.

1672, 1675 JOSEPH CLELAND—Pupil of the ' 4th Class,' 1672, laureated, 1675

1630. LUDOVIC CLELAND—' Primogenitus Domini Jacobi militis.' Takes the oath   (Son of Sir James Cleland of Monkland. This places his birth at about 1617.)

1598, 1600 MATTHEW CLELAND—Takes the oath, 1598; laureated, 1600.

1702. PATRICK CLELAND—Pupil of the ' 3rd Class '

1723, 1725. THOMAS CLELAND—Pupil of the 3rd Class, 1723; laureates (with John Cleland), 1725

1624. WILLIAM CLELAND—Student.

1640. WILLIAM CLELAND—' Ex quinto classe '

1673. WILLIAM CLELAND—Pupil of the 4th Class

1676, 1678. WILLIAM CLELAND—Pupil of the 4th Class on both dates

1681, 1683. WILLIAM CLELAND—Has a Zachary Boyd theological bursary in both these years. (Probably this is the same William Cleland from 1676-1683)

1697. WILLIAM CLELAND—Pupil of the 4th Class.

1838 ALEXANDER BROWN CLELAND—M.D., 1838. Matric., 1831. Sixth son of James Cleland, merchant of Port Glasgow.

1832, 1834 GEORGE CLELAND—' Scotus,' C.M. (1832), M D. (1834)

1840-44. HENRY WILSON CLELAND—Glasgow. Prof of Med. Jurisprudence in Portland Street School of Medicine (1840-42), d 1844, son of James Cleland, LL.D., M D , 1840.

JAMES CLELAND, LL.D , 1826. Cabinet maker in Glasgow, 1790-1814, etc.

JOHN CLELAND, M A , 1777.   ' Filius natu Secundus Mosis Armigeri Comitatu de Down.'

JOHN CLELAND, M.A., 1815. 'Scotus'; according to Oliver and Boyd's Almanac, a person of the same name was at one time Church of Scotland minister at Portland Head and Pitt Town, N S.W.

JOHN CLELAND, B Sc., 1882. Engineer at (1) Airdrie, (2) Glasgow, (3) Kilmarnock.

ROBERT CLELAND, M A , 1808 'Fil n. Max. Roberti in Parochia de Cambusnethan Lanarkshire.'

SAMUEL CLELAND, M.A , 1820. 'Filius natu maximus Davidis Agricolae in parochia de Sainfield in comitatu de Down in Hyb.' (Matric. Alb 1815.)

WILLIAM CLELAND, B.Sc , 1887. (1) Demonstr in Engineering Lab. of Yorkshire Coll., Leeds. (2) Supt of Sheffield Testing Works.

EDINBURGH.

(From Catalogue of the Edinburgh Graduates, 1858)
(M.A 's)

DAVID CLELAND   July 11, 1687. 'Privatim Laurea donati'

GEORGIUS CLELANDUS. July 22, 1637. Class 49 Mr Andreas Stephanides, Regens

GEORGIUS CLELANDUS 1671. Class 83

JOANNES CLELAND. June 22, 1633. Class 45. Mr. Andreas Stephanides, Regens.

JOANNES CLELAND   1669. Class 81 'Nos ingenui Adolescentes,' etc.

JOANNES CRELAND   May, 1685 'Privatim laurea donati'

JOANNES CLELAND. May 12, 1686 'Privatim laurea donati.'

ROBERT CLELAND. 1665

ROBERT CLELAND. 1691. 'Publice Laurea donandi'

WILLIAM CLELAND January 6, 1681 'Publice Laurea donati sunt.'

WILLIAM LENNOX CLELAND   April 1, 1819 Graduated (This Wm. Lennox Cleland is the father of John Fullarton Cleland While studying at Edinb Univ. he first met and afterwards married Miss Fullerton   Gordon-Lennox is the family name of the Duke of Richmond.)

GEORGIUS CLILAND Minister verbi July 29, 1603

JACOBUS CLILAND. Minister verbi. July 30, 1597. (' is this the author of the "Education of a Young Nobleman.")

BIBLIOTHECA CLELANDICA.

1. CLELAND, ARCHIBALD, Surgeon —Appeal to the Public.   London, 1743 8vo —Description of a Catheter, for the High Operation for Stone   Phil. Trans , 1741, Abr. VIII , p. 526 —Needles for Operations in the eyes , Instruments for the ear   Ib., p 528 *(Watt's Biblioth. Brit 1824)*

2. CLELAND, BENJAMIN —Sermon on John xiv , 1-3 , 1607. 8vo. *(Watt s L.bl Brit)*

3. CLELAND, CHARLES.—Abstract of the several Laws and Rules that are now in Force relating to the Importation and Exportation of Wine, into and out of Great Britain London, 1737. 4to. *(Watt's Bibl. Brit)*

4. CLELAND, ELPHINSTONE DAVENPORT —" The White Kangaroo," a boy's story illustrative of Australian Life —Contributions (short stories, etc.) to Australian Press

5. CLELAND, ELIZABETH.—New Method of Cookery. Edinburgh, 1759 8vo *(Watt's Bibl. Brit.)*

6. CLELAND, GEORGE —The best way to shoe . . . horses .   .   . . with practical remarks, by Farrier Cleland 1884 8vo.

7. CLELAND, HENRY —Lite of the Right Hon William Pitt 1807 12mo *(Watt's Bibl. Brit)*

8 CLELAND, HENRY WILSON, M D —On the History and Properties, Chemical and Medical, of Tobacco, a Probationary Essay presented to the Faculty of Physicians and Surgeons, Glasgow, by Henry Wilson Cleland, M.D , Lecturer on Medical Jurisprudence in the School of Medicine, Portland Street (a Candidate for Admission into that Body). 1840 —This is an interesting account of the history of tobacco and the way in which its use spread over Europe prohibitions against it : its medicinal properties, etc This Henry Cleland was a son of James Cleland, LL.D., the Glasgow statistician

9. CLELAND, JAMES, D D.—The Institutions of a young Nobleman, in six books. Oxford, 1607. 4to.—Death and Funeral of Ludowich, Duke of Richmond. London, 1624. 4to. *(Watt's Bibl. Brit)* —Institutions of a young Nobleman —Jacob's Well and Abbot's Conduit, paralleled, preached and applied in the Cathedrall. .   Church of Christ in Canterbury, 1626. 4to. —James Cleland appears to have been for many years a tutor to the sons of various noblemen, and writes this work on retiring from such occupation. It is full of excellent advice as to how to bring up a son, how to direct his studies, what money allowance he is to have, how he is to comport himself in various circumstances, etc. Many of his recommendations might well be followed in the present day In talking of the choice of a name for a son he says .—" I would wish that they give their sonnes, pleasant and easie Names to be pronounced and remembered ; because good names were ever esteemed to be happie, and first enrouled in the Roman musters, first called out to sacrifice at the establishing of Colonies, and ever erected to high honors : as appeareth by Constantine, who of a simple souldier was chose Emperour at Silchester by the armie of the Britains against Honorius, onlie for his luckie name So was one Religianus of no greater quality made Emperour of Illericum. In all contries and nations there hath ever beene some names more affected than others, as James in Scotland, Henry in England, and Charles in Germanie."

10. CLELAND, JAMES, LL D., of Glasgow —A description of the Manner of Improving the Green of Glasgow, of raising water for the supply of the Public Buildings of that City, etc., etc. Glasgow, 1813 8vo.—Annals of Glasgow, comprising an Account of the Public Buildings, Charities and the Rise and Progress of that City. Glasgow, 1816 2 vols, 8vo, 21s *(Watt's Bibl. Brit)* Letter to his Grace the Duke of Hamilton on the Parochial Registries of Scotland 1813.—Abridgment of the Annals of Glasgow, 8vo. 1817.—Rise and Progress of the City of Glasgow, 8vo 1820 —Exemplification of Weights and Measures of Glasgow, 8vo. 1822 —Statistical Tables relative to Glasgow, 8vo; and Enumeration of Scotland, 8vo 1823.—Specification for Rebuilding Ramshorn Church, 8vo; and Account of Ceremonial at Laying Foundation-Stone of First House in London Street, 8vo. 1824 —Historical Account of the Steam Engine, 8vo —Historical Account of the Grammar School of Glasgow, &c., 1825 —Account of Ceremonial at Laying Foundation-Stone of John Knox's Monument, Glasgow. 1825.—Specification for Rebuilding St. Enoch's Church, 8vo; and Poor Rates of Glasgow, 8vo 1827.—Maintenance of the Poor, 8vo. 1828 —Account of Cattle Show at Glasgow, 8vo — Statistical and Population Tables relative to Glasgow, 8vo.— Enumeration of the Inhabitants of Glasgow, 8vo. 1828.— Abridgment of Annals (second edition) 8vo 1829.—The Account of Glasgow, for Swan's views on the Clyde — Enumeration of Glasgow and Lanarkshire, small folio, 1831; a second edition of the same, large folio, appeared in 1832 — Ceremonial at Laying Foundation-Stone of Broomielaw Bridge, 8vo 1832.—Historical Account of Weights and Measures for Lanarkshire, 8vo 1833.—Statistics relative to Glasgow, 8vo. 1834 (Read before the British Association at Edinburgh).— On Parochial Registry of Scotland, 8vo 1834 —Glasgow Bridewell or House of Correction, 8vo. 1835. (Read before the British Association at Dublin) —A few Statistical Facts relative to Glasgow, 8vo. 1836 (Read before the British Association at Bristol.).—The articles " Glasgow " and " Rutherglen " for the New Statistical Account of Scotland, 1838 —The article " Glasgow " in the seventh edition of the Encyclopædia Britannica —The article " Glasgow," for Brewster's Encyclopædia, and likewise a description of that city for the Edinburgh Gazetteer —An Historical Account of the Bills of Mortality and Probability of Human Life in Glasgow, and other large Towns, 8vo 1840 —On the former and present state of Glasgow. 1840. (Read before the British Association at Glasgow)

11. CLELAND, JOHN, M D , LL D , F.R S , Regius Prof. of Anatomy and Physiology, Galway, then Regius Prof. of Anatomy, Glasgow. Books, (1) The Mechanism of the Gubernaculum;

with an Introduction on the Development, and a Physiological Appendix Prize Thesis, Edinburgh. Maclachlan and Stewart, 1856 —(2) Joint Editorship of Quain's Anatomy, 1867 —(3) Directory for Dissection of Human Body. 1st Edition, 1876; 2nd Edition, 1881.—(4) Animal Physiology, 1874 —(5) Evolution, Expression and Sensation, 1812 (in great part a reprint; preface and portion of articles new) —(6) Scala Naturae, 1887 (poems).—(7) Joint Authorship of Cleland and Mackay's Human Anatomy, 1896. Of many important communications to scientific periodicals, the following may be mentioned :—(1) On the Use of Saccharated Lime in Medicine. *Edinb Med Journal*, July, 1860 —(2) On the Relations of the Vomer Ethmoid, and Intermaxillary Bones. *Philosoph Trans*, 1862 —(3) On the Hutchinsonian Theory of the Action of the Intercostal Muscles *Journal of Anatomy and Physiol* , May, 1867 —(4) On the Epithelium of the Cornea of the Ox *Journ of Anat and Physiol.*, May, 1858; and *Quarterly Journ of Microscop. Science*, July, 1868 —(5) Inquiry into the Variations of the Human Skull. *Philosoph. Trans*, 1870 —(6) The Relation of Brain to Mind. Pamphlet, 1882 —(7) Terminal Forms of Life. *Journ. Anat and Phys* , July, 1884 —(8) Birds with Supernumerary Legs, etc *Proc. Glasg. Phil Soc.*, February, 1886.—(9) Pathology of Spina Bifida, in Morton's Treatment of Sp Bif., 2nd Edit., 1887.—(10) Longevity of Textural Elements, particularly Dentine and Bone. *Nature*, Feb., 27th, 1890; etc.

12. CLELAND, JOHN, Surgeon, Perth Died 1836.—In the "Edinburgh Medical and Surgical Journal" about 1830, relates a case of empyema, pointing through the chest, incised and drained.

13. CLELAND, JOHN, son of Col. Cleland, the celebrated fictitious member of the Spectator's Club, described under the name of Will Honeycomb; died 1789, aged 80 —Memoirs of a Woman of Pleasure 1750.—The Way to Things by Words, and to Words by Things 1765 8vo.—Specimens of an Etymological Vocabulary; or Essay, by means of the Analytical Method, to retrieve the Ancient Celtic 1768.—Proposals for publishing by Subscription, the Celtic retrieved by the Analytic Method , or Reduction to Radicals, illustrated by various and particularly British Antiquities.—Memoirs of a Coxcomb — Man of Honour. *(Watt's Bibl Brit)* Timbo-Chiqui, an entertainment in three acts 1738 —Titus Vespasian, a tragedy 1760 —The Ladies' Subscription, an entertainment, 1760.

14. CLELAND, JOHN BURTON.—Contributions to "Australian Medical Gazette," 1901-1903, "British Medical Journal," Dec , 1903.

15. CLELAND, J. YULE —Love and Disbelief, a novel. London Perth, 1890 8vo

16. CLELAND, ROBERT —The Piper of Cairndhu *(Cornhill Magazine)* —
     Inchbracken, a novel 1883 (Wilson & McCormick).—A Rich
     Man's Relatives. 1885 (White) —True to a Type. 1887
     (Blackwood).—Barbara Allan, the Provost's Daughter. 1889
     (Blackwood).—Too Apt a Pupil. 1891 (Blackwood)

17. CLELAND, THOMAS —The Christian's Encouragement to Believe; a
     Sermon on Romans x , 11 1660. 4to *(Watt's Bibl. Brit)*

18   CLELAND, WILLIAM.—A Scotch Poet of considerable talents, was a
     Lieut -Colonel in the year   (sic), in what was called Lord
     Angus' Regiment —Disp. Jurid de Probationibus Traj, ad
     Rh. 1684. 4to.—A Collection of several Poems and Verses
     composed upon various occasions. 1697. 8vo. *(Watt's Bibl.
     Brit.)*

19   CLELAND, MAJOR WILLIAM (of that ilk).—Letter to Pope's Dunciad
     (? his authorship)

20. CLELAND, WILLIAM, 21st of that ilk.—Contributions to the great
     quarterlies in the early part of the 19th century

21. CLELAND, WILLIAM, M D. (of Auchinlea).—Dissertatio Medica
     Inauguralis de Variolarum Insitione. Leyden, 1776 Being
     thesis for M.D. there.

22. CLELAND, WILLIAM LENNOX, M.B., C M.—Contributions to Royal
     Society of S. Australia, etc

23. CLELAND, WILLIAM.—Loved, Lost and Found. Memorial Verses
     1878 -1895 —Joy my Firmament, being motives for life com-
     piled by W. Cleland (of Bootle). London, 1897. 8vo

24. CLELAND, WILLIAM, merchant of Barbadoes —The present state of
     the Sugar Plantations consider'd, more especially that of the
     Island of Barbadoes London, 1714. 8vo

25. CLELAND, ——, M A —History of Greece, Macedonia and Syria
     (from the age of Zenophon to the incorporation of those
     States with the Roman Empire), by W R Lyall, — Cleland,
     etc. 1848, etc.

BIBLIOGRAPHY ON THE NAME OF CLELAND.

Addison and Steele's *Spectator,* Anderson's *Memoir of the House
of Hamilton; Blackwood's Magazine,* Vol I . Blind Harry's *Wallace;*
Burton's *History of Scotland,* Carruther's *Pope's Life and Letters;*
James Cleland's *Lanarkshire Register; Commissary Records of Glas-
gow,* Douglas' *Baronage;* Archibald Forbes' *The Afghan War;* Fraser's
Douglas Book, Gentleman's Magazine, 1735, 1789, Greenshield's *History
of Lesmahago;* Grossart's *History of the Parish of Shotts,* Hamilton
of Wishaw's *Sheriffdom of Lanarkshire and Renfrewshire,* Hunter's
Biggar and the House of Fleming; Sir William Hamilton's *Works—
Review of Thomson's Life of Cullen; Herald and Genealogist* Dec.
1867; Irving and Murray's *Upper Ward of Lanarkshire, Laing
Charters,* Loundes' *Bibliographer's Manual,* Macaulay's *History of*

England, General Mackay's Memoirs (Maitland Club); *Memoirs of Sir Edwin Cameron of Locheill* (Maitland Club); *Munimenta Alma Univ*, *Glasg.,* Nichol's *Anecdotes of Bowyer,* Vols II , VIII; Nichol's *Steele's Correspondence; Nisbet's Heraldry* (1722); *Notes and Queries,* 2nd Series Vols. 2, 5, 3rd Series Vols 9, 10 (1866); Balfour Paul's *An Ordinary of Scottish Arms, Regist. Episcop, Glasg , Reg Exchequer Rolls of Scotland, Reg. Magni Sigilli Reg. Scot , Reg. Privy Council of Scotland,* Renwick's *Glasgow Protocols, Roll of Glasgow Graduates; Roll of Edinburgh Graduates,* Scott's *Minstrelsy of the Scottish Border,* Somerville's *Memorie of the Somervilles,* Shadbolt's *Afghan Campaign,* Swift's *Letters to Stella,* Thomson's *Acts of the Scotch Parliament;* Thomson's *Life of Dr. Cullen;* Watt's *Bibliotheca Britannica;* Welch's *Alumni Westministr.,* Wodrow's *Hist of the Sufferings of the Church of Scotland.*

The compiler is aware that many errors of omission and some of commission will be encountered in this work , the difficulties he has had to encounter have been great, at times insuperable, and he trusts that the reader will be lenient with him.   Those who can supply further information on any points connected with the family history, or are in a position to furnish details of the additions that it will be necessary to make from time to time, he hopes will communicate at once with him through Dr. Cleland, F.R.S., The University, Glasgow

THE END.

9 781015 593244